ONCE A MOTHER, ALWAYS A MOTHER

ON LIFE WITH ADULT CHILDREN

ANNETTE BYFORD

First published in 2022 by
Ortus Press, an imprint of Free Association Books

A CIP Catalogue of this book is available from
the British Library

ISBN: 978-1-91138-369-7

.

Cover design by
Candescent

Typeset by
Typo•glyphix
www.typoglyphix.co.uk

Printed and bound in Great Britain

Für meine Mutter

Contents

Introduction   1
Notes on the Interviews

1 From the centre to the margins   11
Tasks and challenges of being a mother of grown-up
children: from early years to empty nest

2 Newcomers and monsters-in-law   41
The growing family: children's partners, weddings,
divorces etc.
Cultural and sociological angle: images of
mother-in-law in media and literature
Psychological angle: re-activation of
oedipal conflict

3 Becoming a grandmother   73
Becoming a grandmother as developmental task in
a woman's life

4 Like mother like daughter   95
Case studies illustrating transgenerational link in
managing family transitions

5 Me, myself, I   115
Positive re-orientation and coping strategies

CONTENTS

6   Acceptance   133
Disappointment on the way to acceptance

7   Changing Relationships   143
Who cares for whom?
Old age and frailty

Summary and Conclusion   159

Acknowledgements   167

INTRODUCTION

I am the mother of two adult children. When my children were small, I really did think being their mother would somehow progress in easily distinguishable and distinct phases. We would all move from the hard work and joy of their early and middle childhood through the likely to be more difficult time of adolescence. Then, at some time when they were in their early twenties, they would be adults and essentially my job would be done. Probably their leaving home would be difficult at first, but then we would all start relating to each other as adults and that would be it, or so I thought.

As a mother of young children I understood about the importance of secure early attachment, of clear boundaries, of the need to allow them to gradually separate from me. It was important to me that they would know without any doubt that they were loved and could delight, but also that they would learn, the older they got, that not everything is about them only and that we must consider how other people are affected by what we do and how we treat them. As long as that was in place, I thought we had a good chance to emerge as adults who could respect each other and enjoy both our separate lives and each other's company. I suspect that I assumed that this phase of being a mother of an adult "child" would not change in itself very much over the years, maybe only if I reached a truly old age and needed more support. Before then though, I must have thought there would not be too many changes, challenges and hurdles. Clearly families are complicated beasts, and I knew how difficult things could get between members of a family long after childhood was over, but, if I am honest, I must have believed deep down that if your parenting was good enough, this would somehow not happen to you and your family.

With my children now well established in their adult lives I have however gained an awareness of the "on-and-on-ness" of parenting , as the Maggie Smith character memorably describes it in Downton Abbey. I now know that parenting continues in tidal waves, with phases of distance and separateness, followed by phases of intense engagement. Times of relating to each other in a close and harmonious way can be followed by acrimonious struggle; distance can be followed by closeness; times of feeling relaxed about your children's lives can be suddenly interrupted by some news that throws you back into deep worry. You are pulled into renewed engagement and may feel pushed out the next moment. What the right amount of distance is has to be negotiated and renegotiated over and over again. Being a parent of an adult child presents you with more demands for change and more new and varying challenges than I had ever imagined, and, frankly, at times more than I feel sufficiently prepared for.

Obviously every family has their own rhythm regarding these constant adjustments, due to how the lives of all family members evolve. In most families, however, there are certain markers for fairly predictable change where something accelerates or becomes more visible. Your child might move away from home and come back again, but at one point they may settle in a more permanent place. They may move in with a partner, they may get their first more serious job and gain financial independence, or, indeed, they may fail to do so.

There are two events that actually do not only mark an enormous change in our relationship with our adult child, but which even give us a new and different job title. We may not only be a mother anymore, but in addition to that may become a mother-in-law and maybe graduate to grandmother. You may have decided to become a mother, but becoming a mother-in-law or grandmother happens as a result of other people's decisions and actions, and yet it will affect your life and your relationship with your child profoundly.

When my first child was born, I had no immediate family near me, I had no experience of looking after babies nor for that matter the benefit of having anybody around me who did have that experience and who could have passed it on to me. I turned to books. Penelope

Leach's "Baby and Child" was my bible; I found her combination of practical advice and attention to the emotional life of the baby and the mother truly helpful. Once I started to understand what might be going on for me and this little new person, I could ground myself and meet my daughter's needs.

In my current journey through the late stages from motherhood to mother-in-law to grandmother I don't have access either to anybody who could pass on their experience to me. My mother-in-law is dead; my mother is in a care home suffering from dementia. I have some idea how they managed, but I wish I could ask them more about it. I wish there was a similar book to the baby and child books available, not necessarily giving advice, but helping me to understand what is going on. I have not found a single one. Where to start then?

One thing that strikes me is how, just as we became mothers, again at this later stage of motherhood we walk into a storm of expectations, our own and those of other people. There are stereotypes, images, stories and jokes that are embedded in the society we live in, and these will have translated themselves into our family histories and those of our peer groups. We cannot help but expect, fear, predict, and some of it is entirely out of our control. How is it for example that being a mother-in-law creates such immediate negative emotional associations? Why can the mother-in-law provoke such an endless string of hostile jokes, offensive caricature in literature, film, media etc, and yet with the transition to being a grandmother the lighting on the whole changes to soft focus and grandmothers, as a category, gain a completely different associative status?

Another complication is that, in whatever way the changes in our children's lives impact on us and demand adjustment and adaptation in our relationship with them, there are likely to be changes in our own lives too that have essentially nothing to do with them, running in parallel and yet interacting. We might be freed up to pursue our careers without the constant effort of juggling work and family life that characterises life with younger children. Yet we may also experience that a child's demand for us to drop what we are doing when they need us never entirely stops, nor do we necessarily know any better how to respond.

Alternatively, we may near retirement, just when we are adjusting to being increasingly redundant in our children' lives. Or we may look forward to developing a new life, new projects, and then find ourselves drawn back in through the joys and tasks of grandparenthood. We may have to renegotiate our relationship with our partner, when at the same time our children as significant others become more removed. We may have elderly parents with increasing needs or we may have to deal with the death of parents. All these changes mean that we do not just have to learn how to relate to our adult children differently, but we experience ourselves differently. We are not necessarily who we were anymore and change is nearly always hard work.

I am a mother and grandmother, but I am also a psychologist and psychotherapist, so I decided to approach this subject with the tools that I have available: I read, I listened, I analysed and I constructed stories, all of it in an attempt to get hold of the core of the experience of this late stage of motherhood as I observed it around me and inside myself.

The result is this book. It aims, more than anything else, to increase our understanding of what is happening to ourselves and our families at this stage of our lives and to make sense of it. Whilst it certainly is not a straightforward self-help book, it does make suggestions on how we may navigate our way through the pitfalls of each stage on the way.

I would like to invite the reader to follow me along the different avenues of exploration I have chosen, some of which may be more meaningful to you than others:

- The book follows the timeline of stages of motherhood, from early years to children leaving home, through the stage of incorporating children's partners into the family, grandparenthood and eventually the need for adult children's support in advanced old age and potential frailty.

- I have interviewed mothers about their experience of having grown-up children and the results of these interviews form the backdrop to what I have identified as the major features, challenges and experiences of the late stages of motherhood.

- I have looked at the cultural context in which women grow older while their children grow up, paying attention to images of older women, particularly mothers-in-law and grandmothers, as they appear in media, literature and general social discourse. This includes the question of whether different cultures offer women different images and realities of growing older and different roles within their extended families.

- Individual accounts of this stage of motherhood can be more meaningfully understood if they are put into a psychological context that includes intergenerational narratives specific to a particular family. Here I have drawn again from the interviews, but also from psychoanalytic thinking and family therapy.

- Each chapter ends with suggestions of what to look out for on the journey through different phases of our family's and our children's lives and how to cope well with it.

- The reflective parts of the book are interspersed with short stories which put into fiction this intensely personal and often complicated experience, all of them picking up different dimensions of having adult children, offering sketches of women's lives at this stage. They are woven through the more reflective and discursive chapters of the book and can be read on their own or be treated as illustrations of the themes appearing in those chapters.

Notes on the interviews

As part of this project I spoke with about thirty-five women who had volunteered to be interviewed.

Some of the interview material was part of an earlier project on mothers' experience of their child's wedding (the results of which you can see in my book *A Wedding in the Family*); most were new interviews taking the questions that had arisen in the wedding interviews further.

All interviewees had children at various stages of adulthood. I had specified in adverts and informal approaches that I was interested in mothers whose children where older than eighteen and who had at least for a while left the maternal home. As a result I ended up with a group of interviewees whose age range was between early fifties to late seventies, with some of them now having grandchildren. All my mothers lived in the UK. They were from different social and ethnic backgrounds, the majority of the women being white British, but some of them came from South European, South American, Asian and Chinese backgrounds. I am aware that this group did not in any way provide a socially or culturally representative sample. This was a small-scale study and my focus was on getting hold of the quality of emotional processes relevant to the group of interviewees defined by their family status, rather than aiming for anything approaching statistical relevance or making significant statements about the differences due to social and cultural background.

Having said that, it is clear and became apparent in the interviews that cultural and social backgrounds without any doubt influence the expectations of the members of any family as to what roles they are supposed to be playing in their families at various stages of the family's life cycle. What constitutes successful interactions between mothers and their adult offspring varies between national, ethnic and social cultures. Middle class families for example tend to live further away from their offspring which influences the kind of contact they have with each other and what they regard as normal family cohesion. In Asian and Mediterranean cultures the greater importance of extended family compared to friendship networks seems to be accepted and expected and the rules that this creates lead to different accounts of successful or non-successful transitions of children growing up. There are also significant variations between the mini cultures of individual families and what is acceptable in one family may be seen as hurtful or disappointing in another.

However, in my interviews my main interest was in what may run across these cultural differences, what may form part of a core set of challenges and emotional responses that can be observed in mothers beyond those differences. Individual mothers may describe different events as significant in their observation of their child growing up, but the feeling in response to it do not seem to be that different from mother to mother.

Indeed, whilst each woman's story is unique and set in the context of her unique family story, there are themes that come up in all the interviews and provide a link between all these mothers' experiences. It is these shared experiences that I was interested in.

I am aware that I have been trusted with highly personal and at times quite sensitive material and I have therefore taken great care to guard the anonymity of my interviewees. Names, of course, have been changed and biographical details have been changed as much as possible without making the information meaningless. The women may recognise themselves at times, but nobody else should.

Chapter 1

From the centre to the margins: early stages

Short Story

Lisa's Story: Stepping Back

Weddings and stepping back... Why it should go through my head so much I do not entirely know. What I come back to over and over again is this stepping back. That's what you do: you walk her down the aisle, or one of you does anyway, and then you step back. That's the main part of the wedding I think. I hadn't really understood that until recently, not until after the wedding.

A wedding in the family... When I used to say "family", I would think of myself and my husband and our children. Of course, there has always also been "his" family and "my" family, grandparents and aunts and uncles, but they were the second layer somehow. As far as I was concerned, in the middle of my family universe, there were just the two of us and the children. We had family holidays (the four of us), family celebrations (the four of us again, plus maybe his family, or mine, alternating at Christmas: "this year it is my in-laws' turn, next year it's my parents'"). It was not always uncomplicated, certainly those Christmases could be hard work, but on the whole it worked and it felt good and safe to be at the centre of it.

We somehow sailed along over the years, the children grew up: there is one phase, and just when you come to grips with it, there is another one. For years you think, things will get easier when they are older, sleep through the night, get out of nappies, can entertain themselves a bit, can be left with a babysitter, go to school, can explain what is the matter... Things do get easier and before you know it they get harder again. People say they feel broody and they really yearn for a baby, they don't on the whole yearn for a teenager. Mine weren't that bad, they really weren't. I just rather worried about them, as you do. They were just straining at the bit, wanting to explore life outside the family. First it is "but Miss says", then it is "at Emily's house they are allowed" and then "everybody else does". Getting them to come on family holidays became a bit of a struggle. Family was not enough anymore; that hurt, but rather than showing that it hurt, I argued with them about constantly texting and being glued to their phones, their oh so important lifeline linking them to their friends. The inner circle was certainly creaking at the edges. My sister's two kids did not seem to do that. They seemed happy to stay with Mummy and Daddy. I used to feel really envious, but now my sister's children are still hanging around at home, glued to Mummy and Daddy in their twenties, and I would not want that either, definitely not.

I don't really know quite what I want, if I'm honest. I often wonder what my own mother wanted and whether she was happy with how it all turned out. It never occurred to me to ask and it's too late now.

So, children, they grow up, they leave. We helped quite a bit with the first moves and then it got a bit quiet. When my daughter had left, I did some serious cleaning and sorting out, "regaining my space", I said. Then I found her hair scrunchie under the bed and I just cried and cried. I really did not want the mess back, but I wanted her back, "us" back, "our" little family.

I took my eye off the ball for a bit, all our friends' families had got smaller and we got on with it, trying to remember who we had been before we started our family. I often think about that expression now "starting a family". You start a book or a project at work, or you start a list. Then you finish it or you put it aside, unfinished. The family that you start one day, it sort of goes on and on, but it constantly changes shape. You can just sit there and watch it change shape, because certainly the longer it goes on, the less anybody asks you what you think about it all.

They leave home, your family gets smaller and then suddenly they are back again, with all their clutter, and you have to figure out how to live together after all this time, with this child who is both two, and fifteen, and twenty-five at the same time. Then, when you may have just about worked it out, they leave again and you feel grief and relief in equal measures. Then they start bringing people home, boyfriends, girlfriends. You may like them, you may not, it doesn't make much of a difference, not your call after all. Maybe you like them, these newcomers. There was one girlfriend, I loved her to bits. We had such laughs together and the girl seemed to really like me. She certainly was nicer to me than my own children were at times. But then they split up and I never saw her again, just like that. It wasn't my call. I'll be a bit more careful with the next one.

And now we have a son-in-law: I assume that means he is likely to stay around. When they announced they were getting engaged, I felt really quite excited. A wedding, that is exciting, and you would not believe the amount of work and planning that goes into it. I had never been involved in planning such a big party and they do expect something quite grand these days. It is their big day after all.

I was allowed to help and got so caught up in thinking about bunting and balloons and flower arrangements. I collected little jam jars for the flowers on the tables, I started dreaming about jam jars. Looking at venues, thinking about the ceremony, about what to wear, mother of the bride, hat or no hat, about invitations and seating arrangements... It may sound odd, but it was the invitations and seating plans that did it for me in the end. All of a sudden I could see it, there in black and white: there was going to be another family at this wedding and they were from now on going to be my daughter's other family, just like my daughter's husband was going to be my son-in-law. It is quite obvious you may say, but I had just never really thought about it. My "little family" was not just getting bigger, but there was from now going to be this odd overlap with another family. One day there may be grandchildren, and they would belong to my family just as much as they would to this other family. For whom I was now working out a seating plan...

I found it quite difficult to get my head round that one, still do now!

It turned out to be a lovely day, I felt elated for weeks afterwards. We still talk about it a lot, and we get the pictures out and look at them. When my daughter comes round with my son-in-law (still practising saying that!) we often do it together, all four of us. It has become a little joke. One of them will say "What do you think, is it time to *look at the wedding photos again?", and we all laugh and we go through the story of the day and the build up to it again. "Do you remember when Dad said?" they may say, or "do you remember when I nearly forgot, do you remember...?" It confirms it over and over again: we did this together as a family, we shared an experience, we have a similar memory. I like that very much.*

There are loads of official photos, but what I particularly like are the photos of my daughter getting ready. There are shots of her wedding dress, the flowers, but also several shots of my daughter and me "getting her dressed". I know, it sounds rather ridiculous, of course she could get dressed herself, but that is what they call it: you get the bride dressed. I remembered standing behind her, and it so reminded me of when she was a small child: all those times when I combed her hair, before school or some outing, all those plaits and ponytails. I am not quite sure how to describe it, but just in that moment I was transported back there, to my "little family", to my daughter when she was little, when we were so close and I was at the centre of our life together. It was as if I was back there one last time. And yet at the same time I was getting her ready for her new life, where she and her new husband would be at the centre and I would be on the margins. Not unimportant, you understand, just a bit more removed. Then my daughter was ready and I stepped back. As her father did when he walked his daughter down the aisle and then he stepped back too. That was when I cried, at those two moments.

Don't get me wrong, I am so happy for her, and I really would not have wanted her to stay at home and not get on with her life. I am really happy for her, and my son-in-law is a lovely guy after all.

It is so weird how a wedding shows you what is happening in your family and actually what has been happening all this time, right from the beginning: your babies, they start walking, they go to the child minder, they go to school, they make their own friends, they go into town on their own for the first time, on a school trip for the first time, for a sleep-over for the first time, pack their bag and go and don't really think about you that much anymore. They step forward and you step back. This is how it should be, you are supposed to launch them not fly with them.

Maybe now that the wedding is over they start their own family? That is how it should be.

Their turn now and then it will be their turn too for the next bit: for them too to start the long journey of stepping back.

Early days

The wish for a child is often a deeply felt urge, a nearly visceral desire, more often than not tied in with a need to complete something or to repair something about ourselves. It is intrinsically linked with our own experience of having been parented, with our own fantasy of the baby as the missing piece in a jigsaw, necessary for our own "successful" life. We are not likely to even examine this complex web of motives in detail, as the wish of a couple to become parents is seen as the norm. Childlessness is seen as a sad exception, chosen childlessness as something that needs an explanation. You do not on the whole need to explain why you want to become a parent, but you may be asked why you do *not* want to.

So if and when we find ourselves in the position of having to take care of an infant, whether this is what we planned or not, wished for or not, few of us have a true idea of what we have let ourselves in for.

For women in particular, in that emotional, physical and hormonal chaos of early motherhood, there is the need to process the intense attachment that will start to form with this new little person, the sheer weight of the never-ending drudgery of looking after a small infant, but also the first experience of loss. The journalist Eva Wiseman talks of the "love that is only two centimetres away from grief". The new mother is not the person she was before she became a mother, her body will have changed, her relationship with the father of the child will change and the baby, one minute still a part of her own body, has become another, a little being outside of her body whose needs are definitely not identical to her own needs. There is this little creature who does not want to sleep when her mother wants to sleep, be quiet when she wants to be quiet, be alert when she wants to be alert. The new mother will have to learn to read this baby, understand her needs and respond in a way that is specific to this baby. If it works, mother and baby will learn to perform a dance that suits them both. They will develop a deep intimacy which is based on a closeness arising out of a rudimentary understanding that they are two different people. They "learn" each other.

Still at this stage there are moments when boundaries between them blur. Mothers describe the experience of confusion where their own body starts and the baby's body stops; they describe feeling what their baby feels, as if the baby's distress or mood state leaks into them. This is acknowledged as a crucial part of learning to hold and contain a young infant. It is also extremely confusing and hard work. The redeeming feature of this stage of early motherhood is the intense attachment that forms between mother and child. A young baby's passionate attachment is unparalleled in its intensity. It may be an exhausting bind to be so central to somebody that hardly anybody can take your place, but as a mother of a baby and toddler you are as central to somebody else's world as you are ever likely to be.

Early motherhood entails the beginning of a separation: the umbilical cord has been cut and there are two of you, mother and child, but the mother is without any doubt still very much at the centre of her child's emotional and probably practical world. This can feel suffocating and overwhelming, but can also be highly rewarding. Your attention, your praise, your comfort, your loving and responsive gaze, your sheer presence, is all that your baby wants. The dominant task of this phase is to allow for a secure attachment to form in which sensitive and predictable responses between mother and baby are established and form a blueprint for the child's core belief system about the world and the trustworthiness of relationships.

What is clear though is that separation is built into the fabric of motherhood from the very beginning. Mothers need to be able to see their babies as separate and not as an extension of themselves. Being a mother to an adult child is a world away from those early days of looking after a baby, but it is on the same continuum and the task of facilitating our child's growing away from us is present from the word go; it just becomes more visible and more complicated. Lisa in the short story describes it as "stepping back". Maintaining a delicate balance of support and respect for our child's separate identity will become the central task of mothering an adult child, but it starts right at the beginning.

Growing independence: from toddler to teenager

Gradually the world will come into what starts off essentially as a dyad between mother and baby; other caregivers play an increasing part: fathers of course, grandparents, aunts and uncles, childminders etc. The child will become mobile, will want to explore away from mother and increasingly use her as a base from which to explore. Being the charging unit, the mother ship, the base camp; these are images that women have used in their conversations with me, describing this phase of early mothering that seems to be pleasant to most of them in this respect: to watch your child's increasing independence can be very exciting; it frees you up that little bit, but still maintains your importance to the child. The emotional cord that tethers mother and child to each other is still strong and solid, but it allows for increasing separateness. In my interviews with mothers for this project it became clear that differences emerge here as far as the mothers' experience of this stretching of the cord is concerned. Some feel they can breathe again, they feel less engulfed by the bottomless pit of their baby's needs, less overwhelmed by the enormous responsibility of keeping this little creature alive and safe. They describe their child's growing independence as a chance to be their separate self again and embrace their child's launching himself into a wider world with pride, joy and some relief. Others feel disorientated and bereft at the loss of the intimacy of the early days and they feel this loss as the first milestones of separation. Leaving the child with a childminder or at the nursery can become traumatic or it can just be full of a poignant sadness about something being over that cannot be regained. Some mothers describe feeling both at the same time.

Either way, at this stage without any doubt mothers are still the base, they are still firmly positioned at the centre of their child's world with all the pressure and joy that this brings. The scales between being needed and close on the one hand and enjoying some space between each other on the other hand tend to be well balanced at this stage. Successful parenting in this phase could well be measured by the presence of strong and secure attachment which in turn will lead to the child being increasingly confident in engaging with the world away from its emotional launch pad. It is the beginning of a launch though, away from the mother, and it is gathering pace.

Becoming a parent starts you on to a journey of transitions. It is just a phase, you are being told over and over again, and indeed before you have quite caught up with one phase another one arrives. Gradually it becomes clearer that there is no turning back. The child is growing older and the relationship between parent and child gradually changes. The child's increasing independence and the widening of his world has to involve a gradual diminishing of the parent's role and importance. The long journey of separation is accelerating and pride and relief have their shadow side of loss and grief. Love two centimetres from grief...

Most mothers are aware of this and feel it at crucial milestones, the child entering school being the one most often mentioned. Few women do not mention that moment when the classroom door closes and their "baby" has joined another world to which the mother has no access. The teacher, another adult, rules this world of school and becomes important to the child. Hearing "But Miss says" may take mothers aback a little and of course it is not just the teacher, but the child's peers, that become increasingly significant. The child may encounter other families and other family cultures where things are not done the way they are at home. A healthy family will be open to this increased contact with other worlds, but it can also feel threatening in that different perspectives become possible. On the whole the mother's approval, praise and interest are still crucial to the child and mothers are still reassured that their importance and their position in their child's life is enduringly strong. One mother described to me what she saw as the best phase of family life for her:

Elenor has two children under twelve, both she and her husband work: *"At the end of the day everybody has been somewhere else and then everybody comes back home and we have got something to tell each other and we are pleased to be together because we have been allowed to be away from each other for a while. That felt good".*

Freud talks of the latency stage of child development, meaning the time between about six years and the onset of puberty, as a relatively peaceful phase of stability. Indeed that is how it can often feel for the whole family with the balance between closeness and separate independence potentially working well for all family members. It is the later storm of adolescence that tends to upset this balance and indeed must upset it in order to prepare for the next big step of separation.

This however is still the phase in which mother and child practise how to be safely separate with the physical, social and emotional umbilical cord gradually being stretched. To experience that people can be away from each other and yet stay linked and connected, to experience that one's own capacity to deal with the world and its joyful and painful offerings is growing, that survival and becoming who we are can be supported by those who love us and who will neither hold us back for their own needs, nor push us away before we are ready: those experiences can be facilitated or thwarted at this stage. "Giving them roots and giving them wings" may strike some as a bit of a corny phrase, but it captures this double task.

Adolescence

With the onset of adolescence separation now becomes a major feature of the relationship between mother and child.

Adolescents want to spread their wings, often before their mothers are ready for it, often before their mothers think their children are ready for it, and the resulting conflict characterises most of the interaction between mothers and children at this stage. What may have felt like a relatively smooth transition so far now becomes rapid, jerky, and often conflict-ridden. The comedian Harry Enfield captures the sudden shock of the change at this age in an episode of his TV series "Kevin and Perry go large" when the child Kevin turns thirteen and morphs into a teenager overnight, leaving his parents utterly bewildered. Swinging between wanting to be seen as grown up and wanting to scuttle back at least momentarily into earlier childhood characterises the adolescent's relationship with his parents. From being adored, needed, sought out as a source of comfort, encouragement and support, mothers find themselves on the receiving end of a hot and cold treatment, having to tolerate being looked at through suddenly hostile eyes. This is a dramatic fall from grace that can feel excruciatingly painful. Many times I heard mothers in the interview refer to *"that look"* that their adolescent child, particularly their adolescent daughters, may give them and it is a look that is a complete reversal of that adoring gaze of early childhood. The mother's gaze is supposed to mirror something back to the child: containment, delight, calming and exciting, encouraging and supporting. However the small child's gaze also mirrors something back to the mother: here she is at least for a while the most beautiful, lovable, important person on the planet. At least to her child she is endlessly funny, exciting and beguiling. That is a far cry from "that look" that an adolescent can give you, *"as if I was something the cat brought in"* as one mother put it, a look that can be bored and dismissive, even hostile or disgusted. Mothers' resources of sense of self, self-confidence and sense of humour will be sorely tested. At the same time they may worry about the kind of person their child is morphing into and the choices their child makes with decreasing consultation with their parents. Mothers described to me the anxieties of this phase, understanding the need to allow their teenagers more freedom and independence, but worrying intensely about the implication of some of the choices their child may make. Could they afford to step back? Would they be negligent if they did or interfering if they did not?

Some mothers may find it very challenging to even imagine a kind of mothering that does not consist only of "mummying" as they were used to with their much younger child.

Alison describes how much she still does for her adult son who has recently moved back home: *"I know I should hold back a bit, not do everything for him, the moment he wants it, but I feel I ought to, if I want to be a good mother. I feel guilty if I don't."*

For other mothers, letting their child find their own way, letting them make their own mistakes even, is too anxiety provoking and challenging.

On one end of the scale you can see extreme helicopter parenting with parents micromanaging their child's life and stifling any healthy space for experimenting. On the other end of the scale there may be an abdication of parental responsibility, expressed through both lack of boundaries and unavailability. Fear may play a part in *both* parental responses: fear of losing control in the first group or fear of confrontation in the latter. Behind both looms the realisation of the prospect of the adolescent growing away, making choices that increase the gap between parent and child, with the ultimate danger of loss of the child and any relevance the parent may have in their life.

Here we have the core fear and the core conflict that characterises so many later interactions between mothers and their growing up and grown-up children. In my interviews with mothers concerned with the experience of having adult children, adolescence is the phase of parenting that many of them come back to over and over again as the one when everything changed and the landscape of being a mother of an adult child was beginning to take shape. Mothers may play down what happened when their children became teenagers, they may have had a relatively easy time with it or they may see it as an interruption of an otherwise harmonious relationship that settled after the stormy phase of adolescence. Either way they all can still remember the shock, challenge and fear of it.

Bryony's account of her daughter's teenage years during which Bryony herself was a single parent captures this well. She talks about the shouting, the *"shocking physicality of the conflict"* with her daughter. *"She would just exit the house, the window would swing open and she would try to get out and I would grab hold of something of her and pull her back."*

There is in her recollection a moving description of her lying next to her daughter all through the night when she has been brought home drunk, holding her like a baby trying to keep her safe. She comments on the *"passion"* of it and sheer madness.

"We all felt like babies at the end of it."

She remembers her daughter's teenage years as a terrifying regressive space that swallowed both of them up, leaving her with the fear that:

"We might not come out of this ok."

Bryony, like other mothers, is aware that this particular daughter "presses buttons" the way another child might not, a theme that will be explored further.

Others talk of their fear and helplessness watching their child engaging in risk-taking behaviour, being terrified at the time or regretful afterwards at what they perceive as their failure to protect their child. The saddest stories I heard in the interviews were the ones where mother and child did indeed not "come out of this ok" in the end. Some of them spoke of clearly very damaged relationships between themselves and their child which had not recovered after adolescence. Others described how their child's risk-taking behaviour during the teenage years turned out to be the precursor of ongoing struggles with mental health issues and destructive and chaotic choices in their later adult life. I heard of mothers losing contact with their children, searching for them and finding them in desolate places, of adult children living in abusive relationships, estranged from their parents, of addiction and other forms of self-harm, with the mothers as helpless bystanders.

Charlotte who lost contact with her adult son for a couple of years tells me how she finally traced him and got access to the room he lived in.

"I had never seen such a tip in my life, just a mattress, and dirty clothes and bottles. You could not see the floor. There was a tin of dog food with a fork in it."

Doreen's son is now an alcoholic and she sees him in the town she lives in on park benches and in doorways. She has after a long struggle decided not to give him money any more, as she understands this would not help, but she still buys him a pair of shoes from time to time.

Several mothers described their helplessness in the face of their adult children's choice of abusive partners.

For most mothers however the difficult teenage years turn out to be "just a phase" indeed, yet the pain, fear and rage this "phase" can create is still very visible in the interviews.

There are those mothers who have a relatively easy time with it. They may just talk about the sense of slight surprise and confusion when the child makes decisions that are clearly the child's rather than the mother's, thus bringing it home to them that their role is changing and their importance waning.

Anne recalls her son deciding to go to the secondary school which she would not have chosen for him. She supports him in his decision, but is aware of the slight sense of shock at the newness of the situation.

Gemma describes how she gradually realised during her children's teenage years: *"I am not everything any more. That's not too hard as long as they are ok."* She finds it very hard though *"if they go to somebody else for help and advice."* Now that they have grown up she says: "*With an adult child, the crucial interaction is behind you, this is what it is now. There is a certain sadness.*"

Bryony says mournfully: "*The little child has gone so suddenly.*"

Laura describes the difficulty of "*the change from having the authority and control to not having it*", but she says the most difficult thing was "*the loss of the child he was*". She likens the constant task of stepping back to an "*ongoing low-key bereavement*".

It was interesting talking with a couple of mothers whose children had gone to boarding school and who reported much less distress during this time. Maybe the conflict is handled somewhere else, maybe the separation has already happened at an earlier stage. One mother interestingly likened being the parent to a child at boarding school to being a grandparent.

"*You do the nice stuff, then you hand them back.*"

Nearly all of the mothers comment on the sense of losing control over events during their child's adolescence whilst at the same time experiencing the relationship becoming more distant and even hostile. For some of them there is only the sense of a slight distance developing in which they feel less and less important. Some feel increasingly like being dismissed as not knowing anything, being old fashioned or just plain irrelevant. Others report being viewed as the enemy and being on the receiving end of hostile attitudes and behaviour.

Some mothers handle this as part and parcel of their child's growing up and with the help of a sound sense of humour can often enjoy their child's growing independence. Others suffer greatly from the rejection they feel for themselves and from the fear they may feel for their child. It is perhaps not surprising that these two strands running in parallel can make it extremely difficult to keep things in proportion, to assess how great the danger actually is and how much risk-taking comes as part of normal adolescent territory. It is equally difficult to assess how much the rejection the mothers feel is just another phase, a necessary part of separation. Of course there are many reasons why adolescents feel, think and act the way they do, but I am for the purpose of this book concerned with the parental, particularly the maternal, reaction to this. As one mother put it,

> *"It is like a partner, a husband, a lover leaving. Of course there are differences between a child and an adult partner, but it was a passionate relationship I had with my daughter, there had been and was that great love, and all of a sudden she did not seem to want it at all any more. That knocks you for six and it is ever such hard work to stay the adult here and remember what that is and what that isn't."*

> Leslie: *"When my daughter left, I missed her, the grief... it was not a transition I had chosen and it marked an end."*

The "love centimetres from grief" has now broken through to the grief and can bring so much confusion and rage with it, just when the parents need to keep their wits about them, in order to "stay the adults here".

What many mothers comment on is one other particular quality of adolescence that is characterised by the hot/cold nature of the interaction with parents. A mother of a young child might still have been able to ring-fence "quality time" when it suited her and on the whole be relatively sure that her child would be available. This has now changed drastically. A teenager will have moments where they want to talk, to be close, to be mothered, but those moments are far and few between and they need to be grabbed when they appear.

Linda: *"One minute she is fifteen going for twenty-five, the next minute she wants to cuddle up and be a baby. You have to guess what age they are, right now, at this moment. She can shed years on holiday, getting all silly and playful, or around Christmas, when she wants her stocking and everything exactly as it has been since she was little, and the next minute it is: 'Excuse me? MY life!' It would be funny, if it wasn't so exhausting."*

Mothers have to learn to respond to the on/off commands of the teenager's mood states and needs, they have to "re-learn" their child all over again.

Lucy tells me that she felt there was *"such an odd tension: you are aiming for them to become independent, but then they do it in such unpredictable ways"*.

It is particularly this on/off-ness of connection which seems to continue into all the following phases of relating to the by now grown-up child. In fact, if there is one thing that all the mothers in the interviews agreed on, it is that this process of constant negotiating and renegotiating closeness and distance continues for the rest of their relationship with their adult child. As far as the mothers are concerned there is no doubt that it is the adult child who is increasingly in charge of this negotiation and mothers may feel that they are struggling not to be repeatedly out of step with their child. With the child's independence growing and the struggle of adolescence gradually coming to an end, mothers now find themselves increasingly on the receiving end of their children's decisions.

Early adulthood and first leaving home

At some stage after adolescence is over, most adult children will leave home. "Flying the nest" is a phrase used across cultures, but cultural backgrounds influence the meaning and timing of this. Anglo-American and northern European narratives of successful growing up place great emphasis on "launching" the child with the physical and emotional separation that is supposed to take place for young adults in their twenties. This is not such a central part of the growing up narrative in, for example, southern European and Asian narratives. In Asian and Mediterranean families it is more often regarded as the norm that the adult child stays at home until the point when they get married and start their own family. Interviewees from such backgrounds agree in their description of children growing up which is not so much associated with the ritual of moving out of the parental home that is typical in northern European cultures.

> Aisha: "*If you live at home in your twenties in England, people ask, what is wrong, what is the reason. In my country those questions are asked, if you don't live at home when you are in your twenties and single. It is much more the norm.*"

> Amrita: "*Family is one of our core values. For the child to come back home as a young adult, that is a change, but it's not abnormal. You wouldn't feel in the slightest bit embarrassed about it.*"

Even if the child moves out, there may be stronger parental involvement in their lives throughout their twenties, as described by a Chinese interviewee who commented on her own position falling between traditional Chinese parenting styles and Western parenting styles.

> Huian: "*A lot of my friends in China, they don't step back enough.*"

This taps into a wider issue of growing up possibly not involving the same degree of separation from the family of origin in those cultures. Family often tends to mean the extended family and even after marriage the ties with this extended family may stay stronger or are expected to stay stronger. Family is definitely not just the nuclear family, but rather the "clan", as one of my (Spanish) interviewees put it. This influences expectations of how growing up and separating on the one hand and staying connected with the extended family on the other hand can be managed. This question becomes particularly relevant when children settle with partners or become parents themselves and this will be discussed in chapters 2 and 3. At this stage of early adulthood it is often rather a question of expecting a young adult child still to live in the parental home and potentially have less of a separate life.

In the UK most white British families however will expect their child to move away from the parental home once they have reached their twenties. Many of the mothers I spoke with do remember a particular event which for them signalled that their child was actually growing up and in fact now leaving home: they may remember their child packing their boxes moving into their first shared flat, maybe the journey to university, finding themselves on the motorway passing other cars full of suitcases , duvets and pot plants, maybe with a visit to Ikea somewhere on the way, or the moment at the airport waving their offspring off for their gap year travel. They remember that moment of leaving their child, their son or daughter often keen for them to go now and leave them to it. It may be a planned moment, prepared for and jointly managed, or the result of a less well managed conflict. Either way, mothers do remember that moment. They talk of a raw grief that takes them by surprise in its physical force.

> Sally, whose son left home for university at eighteen, talks of coming home after their journey to his hall of residence: "*When we came home, I went into his bedroom and smelt his pillow and could not stop crying.*"

The mothers I spoke with talk of a sense of confusion about their role in life, now that being a mother does not keep them busy and does not hold them together in the same way that it did before. The "empty nest" is felt by many of them to be an image for a loss that leads to a kind of grief that takes some time to work through.

Others talk of relief, of not needing to be in the grip of constant worry.

> Jenny's son has lived away from home in another city for a couple of years now: "*I just don't know when he is coming home and where he is, and in a strange way that lets me off the hook, there is just nothing I can do. I can actually forget about him for stretches of time, I marvel at that! I did not think that would be possible.*"

What makes things more complicated is the fact that their child leaving home is rarely a one-off transition; it rather happens in a long series of transitions, comings and goings, moving out and moving back. Many mothers comment on the fact that when they themselves left home, that was it and they never moved back in any meaningful sense of the word. They moved out and from then onwards the parental home became a place to visit. Economic conditions have changed that fundamentally. A recent study at Loughborough University found that nearly two thirds of childless single adults aged twenty to thirty-four have either never left or have moved back into the family home due to a combination of precarious job market conditions, low wages, high private sector rents and life shocks such as relationship break-ups. The study found that there has been an increase of about 30% in single young adults living at home over the last decade, which will without a doubt increase further due to the effects of the pandemic. From 70% in their early twenties to 30% in their early thirties of single young adults shared a home with their parents. Often this takes place as a dipping in and out process, complicating the transition for both parents and young adults.

The increase in young adults still living with their parents, even in families where this would not be the cultural norm but rather as a result of economic conditions, and in particular the continuing change between moving out and moving in, has huge implications for the management of the separation process for both parents and children. As this book focuses on the parental, specifically maternal, side of the experience, it is those aspects that I am concerned with. It seems that the child's moving out is for most mothers an indicator of the child's adult status. The child's absence from home allows her to recognise her child as adult and herself as the mother of an adult. The "bounce back" effect confuses the recognition of the child as adult and many descriptions of children moving back home are accompanied by complaints from both sides that time seems to have gone into reverse and both parties regress into a state of relating to each other that does not recognise any more that both parties have moved on. Children often seem to expect "home" to stay as an unchanged space with at times quite marked protests against changes to routines that they have been attached to (note the earlier quote about Christmas rituals) or particularly to "their" rooms.

> One daughter, when seeing that her parents had redecorated her room and wanted to use it as a general guest room in her absence, is reported to have exclaimed: *"Fine, fine, as long as it's clear it's still my room."*

On the other hand, adult children may feel irritated by their mothers' outdated attempts to mother them as if they had not become adults leading an independent life. What mothers of "boomerang" children deal with is many-fold: the bouncing back effect may make it easier to deal with the grief of the separation, as the child has not really left at all, and the mothers have longer to adjust. It also can slow down the process of separation and create a confusing regression. Potentially it deprives the mothers of the relief and release from responsibilities as described by some.

To wave good-bye to your offspring, however challenging and painful it may be, after all also offers you the chance to rethink what you may want to do with the rest of your life, a re-evaluation and re-setting of priorities, professionally and personally. It allows you to remember your pre-mother self and opens the possibility of seeing and thinking about the person you want to be and the life you want to live in your later years. (See more on this in chapter 4.) Leaving home may be an important developmental step for the young adult, but it also is for the parent, and the "bounce back" effect does not necessarily make that any easier.

The major adjustment for the mother, with the child moving from the teenage years to actually leaving home and then gradually establishing a life away from the parental "home", is the increasing need to step back, as described in the short story at the start of this chapter. From the moment that the young person is moving their life away from the parental centre, they also increasingly take control of their own affairs. Decisions are being made by the son or daughter that are not necessarily discussed with the parents any more. The time of seeking permission or even just wanting an opinion is gradually fading. One minute there may have been rows about what the appropriate time is for coming home at night, the next minute career decisions are being made, friends and partners are chosen, wise or unwise purchases are being made without the parents having any particular role in it. Of course families differ greatly; indeed children within the same family differ greatly as to at what speed and to what extent this process unfolds. The trend is however the same in nearly all families and mothers comment on it. Most of them see it as an inevitable and indeed a desirable aspect of their child reaching true independence; indeed they worry if it does not seem to happen and the child shows little inclination to fly the nest.

Julia observes: *"From not being able to survive without us, they move to surviving well without us, that's if we have done our job well."*

Another mother says, *"We can't be certain of their need for us. The happier they are the less they need us."*

If mother and adult child achieve a state of separation that is acceptable to both sides, if they establish full lives away from each other, then the constant dance of moving towards each other and stepping back again can become gradually easier and smoother for both parties and can lead to enjoyable and rewarding contact. Often there is a phase not that dissimilar to the latency phase of middle childhood, providing a bit of a less dramatic lull.

Kate's daughter has settled in a flat of her own within driving distance from her mother: *"I love meeting her for lunch somewhere and we can talk the way I can talk with my friends."*

Amy occasionally visits her son in the town where he has now worked and lived for a while: *"It is such a pleasure to see him in his environment, so competent and easy with people."*

The same goes for Christine: *"Getting together now is a special treat."*

More often than not, however, mothers were describing relationships with their adult offspring that were characterised by the need to watch very carefully where their children positioned themselves at any moment in time and to adjust their behaviour accordingly. They often expressed a rather tired awareness of having to be careful, because any misjudgement of the situation could lead to conflict and misunderstandings. This was particularly a feature of mother/daughter relationships.

Jayne observes: "*When you say something they are likely to hear it as judgement, when all you want to say is, are you sure? Is this right for you?*"

Nicole says: "*It's often like treading on eggshells.*"

Eleonor thinks: "*There is little you can do, it's best to just go along with things.*"

Trisha has come to the conclusion: "*If you say something wrong there will be sanctions. It's better to keep your mouth shut.*"

This dynamic indicates that in the mothers' experience the power has shifted over to their adult child, a process that started in adolescence and has now become firmly established.

All mothers agree that the transition to this new separated stage is not always easy.

Tina describes the feeling that at best she may be, as her son's mother, "*close to the inner circle*" (meaning in this context her son's wife and child) "*but not in the inner circle any more. I feel like an observer to his life rather than a participant.*"

Like many of the other mothers she is trying to define where exactly her place is on this observer/participant continuum:

"*You can't just be an observer, if only because their decisions impact on you.*"

So where to position yourself? Here are just a selection of statements that are made by various mothers in the interviews:

"*I could be a resource.*"

"*I want to be useful.*"

"I would like to have a part to play."

"I want to have a function."

"I don't want to be irrelevant to their life."

The expressed aim for most of them is to find a position between being interfering and overpowering on the one end of the scale and redundant to irrelevant on the other end.

One mother describes her position like this:

"You have all the worry but none of the power," adding, *"You spend years looking after them, caring for them, it doesn't just turn off."*

The worry that this mother refers to is no doubt part of deeply caring about the child well beyond their younger years and holding on to a certain protectiveness. Beyond that it is powerfully maintained by the emotional and practical on/off-ness of the interaction between mother and adult child as mentioned above. Even for those mothers for whom the practical leaving process was fairly straightforward and uninterrupted, there seems to be always something going on that mirrors the on/off nature of the physical bounce back of young adults moving out of home and then back again. Degrees of involvement seem to be in constant need of setting and re-setting for <u>all</u> mothers, independent of degrees of physical separation.

Mothers feel that they continue to be expected to make constant quick changes from observer to participant status, depending on what is going on in their child's life at any given point in time. Nearly all the mothers I spoke with had tales to tell of adult children coming to them with practical or emotional problems. Mothers tend to not mind that and in fact often cherish being needed once more.

Tina tells me of her son wanting to talk with her after a painful breakup from a long-term girlfriend.

"It is difficult to feel I'm barely in his world, irrelevant. So when he was very upset and he turned to me... I was so glad he came to me with it."

However, particularly those mothers who had managed to regain independence from their child and their own maternal identity, having built up a different focus in their lives, expressed a certain amount of wariness at those sudden calls for maternal help. Moving back in with the parents for example may not be easy for the son or daughter, but the mother's privacy and space are also invaded.

Being asked to help with childcare, with finances, being asked to provide practical and emotional support, can happen at any time. An adult child's crisis may coincide with the mother's own work project or holiday or health crisis, and yet most mothers felt that they had to respond and indeed respond promptly, often dropping everything at short notice. They confessed to feeling guilty if they could not or would not do so. One mother went as far as announcing that she was going into an official retreat in her own house for a period of time, with strict instructions to her daughters not to contact her:

Trisha: *"I said don't contact me, unless it is serious enough that you would expect me to book a flight to come back home if I was abroad."*

For this mother it seemed near impossible <u>not</u> to make herself available otherwise.

Managing this on/off quality of being in each other's lives, being expected to switch between participant and observer role, requires a constant renegotiation of the status of separation achieved between mother and adult child which will characterise their relationship for decades to come.

What to do and how to be?

How to get it right? That is of course the question that bewildered mothers ask themselves. What can we watch out for at this stage of our children entering adolescence and then "flying off"?

- Did I get it right with my children? Certainly not a lot of the time! Maybe that is the first thing we could tell ourselves as mothers negotiating these difficult transitions: we will not get it right a lot of the time and we may need to give ourselves permission to make mistakes. The transition from mother of a small child through their teenage years to them leaving home, however gradually or suddenly, is emotionally and practically hugely challenging. A lot is at stake and our coping resources are sorely tested. Trying to be super mum is not a brilliant idea at the best of times; at this stage it inevitably sets you up for failure.

- It seems to me the most important thing is to accept the fact that things will have to change. Successful parenting must lead to increasing degrees of separateness. This <u>will</u> hurt, but trying to hold back the tide is doomed to failure for both mother and child. Try to embrace the positive aspects of it. Your teenager is trouble: good, he is meant to be in order to manage his separation from you. You are feeling useless or alienated and criticised: good, he is doing what comes with this separation, he needs to overdo the breaking of idealisation at least for a while in order to make space for himself. She is getting herself into dodgy situations and makes dodgy decisions and you cannot influence that any more the way you used to: good, she needs to have some space to make her own mistakes in order to learn from them. She does not talk to you anymore the way she used to: does she talk to others, friends etc.? Good, she is taking what she learned in the relationship with you and is transferring it into other worlds, as you know deep down she must! Keep an eye on it, of course, but don't assume you can reverse the trend. You will lose.

- Don't take it personally. This sounds utterly impossible in the hurtful barrage of hostilities that can accompany living with an adolescent. This is not necessarily about you as a person or you as a mother. You could be a saint and your sainthood would be what irritates your adolescent. She does not necessarily mean you, but you fill a vacancy that demands to be attacked. It is not about you failing, but about them needing to distance themselves, and sometimes the closer you were, the greater the need for more violent distancing.

- Link up with support: do not try to do this on your own. You are likely to feel so much loss, rage, confusion, and there is a temptation to feel that it is something that just happens to you and shows your individual failing. Be honest about it with at least some people who you know to be supportive. If nothing else, you will find that you are by no means as alone as you may fear you are.

- Keep your sense of humour! Adolescents can be very funny to be with, voluntarily but also inadvertently. A friend's daughter came home from university for the first time at Christmas. Everybody had been hugely looking forward to seeing her and her mother had spent a lot of time thinking what her daughter might like to eat, preparing meals, imagining how she would like being looked after again after months of student living. As it turned out my friend's daughter spent a major part of the Christmas holidays telling her mother that in student halls she would do things differently, including eating at different times. She actually prepared her own food to eat much later at night and would only occasionally sit down with the family for a meal, telling everybody again that at uni she did things differently. Clearly it was enormously important to tell her mother and herself that things had now changed and she lived her life differently. However, my friend felt very upset and increasingly irritable. We now laugh about the story and she wishes she had been better able to see how these interactions had been on one level so absurd and funny. That might have brought the emotional temperature down a bit!

- Know yourself, because they do know you and they know how to press your buttons. More on that later.

- When they are gone, they have not necessarily gone: prepare yourself for a long period of transition. They may come back when you least expect it, but even if they don't, you both have to learn how to relate to each other in a new and different way. There is no way that you will get this right straight away. After all, they don't know either quite where you are supposed to figure in their life. It may be unsettling, but it is a situation in flux and a bit of patience with yourself and them will go a long way.

- Remember your own separate self. It is not just your adolescent or adult child who is gradually leaving in order to be themselves away from you. You are also more than this child's mother and this may be your chance to link up with who you were before you became a mother, your chance to think about what you want to be when being your child's mother is not at the centre of your own world either.

Chapter Two

Newcomers and monsters-in-law

The next challenge in the family life cycle is often the point at which the adult child settles down with a serious partner. Maybe there have been girlfriends and boyfriends before, but they may have been transitory. There may still have been the sense that these newcomers to the family may come and go, but essentially somehow the original family is still the main unit.

Bryony talks of *"making room at the table for them"*.

The table here is still firmly the mother's table hosting her family and their guests.

At some stage that changes. Maybe there is a wedding, the arrival of a grandchild, or there is just a noticeable shift in attitude in the young couple that signals that they are now the "core unit", with the mother moving gradually into the position of the "guest". Tina describes how this became clear to her when she visited her son and his partner for the first time in their flat and realised by the way the young woman allocated her a room for the night that this was the couple's place and she, Tina, was a guest, a guest who was made welcome, but a guest nevertheless. This was the young woman's space.

"I was close to the inner circle, but not in the inner circle anymore."

Many mothers observe like Tina:

"Now that they have partners there is less intimacy for me with them."

So what are the tasks and challenges of this particular transition?

Weddings

There is one event that marks this transition in a particularly visible and ritualistic way, namely the wedding.

When I researched weddings a couple of years ago for my book *A Wedding in the Family*, I gained an insight into the depth of emotions that an event like a wedding can create for families. People often comment with a degree of surprise on the strength of their own and other people's emotional reactions to what seem to be quite innocuous triggers in the context of a wedding and its preparations. They are often at a loss to explain quite why this should have happened. I think weddings are such powerful events because they stand at a turning point of a family's life cycle, marking the transition of an adult child moving into a different position vis-a-vis their family of origin. As such they hold a significant position concerning the subject matter of this book. Weddings are one of the few remaining rites of passage in Western society, marking through a carefully choreographed ritual a transition for both the wedding couple and their families. They are at the heart of the transition that this chapter is concerned with: mothers and their families have to perform and emotionally process a ritual that demonstrates to them and other observers that their child is now committing to their new partner as their first significant other. The parents are officially stepping back into the second line (see

Lisa's story in chapter 1). Particularly in Western societies, the assumption is that the ties between husband and wife in the new couple are going to be central and are going to supersede the claims of the extended family of origin. Especially in societies where the leaving home has been a slower and more drawn-out process, a wedding marks and makes visible a new boundary between the wedding couple and their respective families. All my interviewees, including those who came from cultures where less emphasis is put on the separation process for single adult children in their twenties, mentioned weddings as the turning point where separation and greater independence of the adult child would be expected and accepted.

There is a complicating factor at this point: at that very same moment when mothers have to come to terms with this new boundary between themselves and their child, symbolised in public by the wedding, another family, their child's in-law family is stepping forward, making a claim to being this new couple's family in their own right. Family boundaries are thus being stretched: mothers have to welcome a new person into their family, the new son-in-law or daughter-in-law. At the same time they are seeing their child join another family.

This transition can stir up feelings which a lot of mothers in my study found surprising. The newcomer to the family may well have been part of their life for quite a while, yet the wedding brings his or her family into view in a new way. Territorial issues and jealousy are a universal undercurrent at all weddings, not an indication of dysfunctional families. They can be managed better or worse depending on a variety of factors present in the two families.[1]

What became very clear in my research around weddings was the fact that at the core of "wedding stress", which at times seemed to be provoked by trivial details, there was a fear on the part of

---

1 Byford, Annette (2019): A Wedding in the Family. London

the mothers that not only might they lose their child to the new partner, but perhaps more significantly also to the "other family". The long process of the child leaving home has come to a crucial junction and details of the wedding can reassure or ring alarm bells: how involved in the preparations are the parents allowed to be, who gets invited and who does the inviting, who pays for what, who sits where, where is the wedding being held, which family is experienced as the dominant one? All these factors are often felt to indicate a direction of travel and mothers react to them as pointers towards their future position in their adult child's life and family. This became particularly visible around the question of mothers of brides and their potential role as "hostess" of the wedding, as old traditions would prescribe. Traditions are changing and it is increasingly the wedding couple rather than the parents who determine the format of the wedding. Nowadays mothers are often struggling to know what role they are supposed to play at a wedding. Both mothers of grooms and mothers of brides were often describing themselves as "special guest" rather than hostess, thus marking their transition from the centre of their child's life towards a more marginal role, with the power increasingly based with the adult child and their partner. This is a far cry from Bryony's "making room at the table" for a child's partner. Now the mother has to wait and see how much room is being made for her. In fact the continuous assessment of a son's or daughter's partner and their attitude towards their new family, combined with a degree of vulnerability on the mother's side, characterises the developing relationship. The question mothers ask themselves is: where is the new boundary going to be between me and my child? How much will I have to relinquish? In other words: how much room will be made at the table for me? Mothers may watch this process unfold or they may try to influence it; either way it is likely to be associated with a degree of uncertainty and anxiety. A wedding is an event when this becomes visible, but it will have been an ongoing process for a while.

Sons-in-law and daughters-in-law

What active roles do the newcomers play in this?

Many women I talked with confirmed the informal impression that gender plays a powerful part in this. Women in our society play a greater part than men do in maintaining and shaping intergenerational relationships. It does therefore potentially make a difference whether the newcomer is a son-in-law or daughter-in-law. There is some support for the saying that "a daughter is a daughter all her life, but a son is a son till he takes him a wife". Various research suggests that there is a greater tendency for sons to step back from or disengage from their family of origin after their marriage than for daughters. In connection with this the continuation of a close relationship between a mother and her adult child after the child's marriage depends on the new spouse to a greater extent for sons than it does for daughters. In other words, in general a daughter-in-law seems to influence the relationship between her husband and his parents in a more powerful way than a son-in-law does regarding his wife's relationship with her parents. What is going on here?

Daughters-in-law often take on the task of "kin-keeping", remembering birthdays, initiating and organising family get-togethers, sending photos of grandchildren to their husband's family in a way that sons-in-law rarely do.

> Paula remembers the early days of her own marriage: "*Once we got married, my husband stopped writing to his mother and I was supposed to take over.*"

> Bryony describes her daughter-in-law as "*the instigator of family group things.*"

Daughters-in-law may actually strengthen the bond between mother and son that may have faded during the years of early adulthood.

Helen says about her daughter-in-law: *"She warms your heart. Just seeing her makes me feel good. She has brought a lot of emotionality into our family."*

Diane says her daughter-in-law *"brought our son back to us"*.

Rachel feels very comfortable with what she calls her daughter-in-law's *"family networking"*. *"She instigates a lot of family group things."*

If the daughter-in-law, however, for whatever reason withholds this kind of kin-keeping, her husband is less likely to maintain the degree of contact with his parents in the same way as daughters do. Mothers are aware of this risk and anxieties are close to the surface.

Paula feels: *"She [daughter-in-law] keeps us at arm's length and he [son] now rings occasionally from his car and thinks he has done his duty."*

Ruth observes anxiously: *"She is bound to be closer to her own family, I can sense that already and her family are quite domineering."*

Helen notices: *"Now that he [son] is with her, there is less intimacy between us."*

Claire confesses: *"I have feared that all of my life, that the girls will take my sons away, you know, where only the family of the girl matters."*

Val: *"She won't come and stay with us. Why would she? She wants to be with her own family. When I go to stay with them... their house is always cold."*

Altogether, daughters-in-law as newcomers to the family have a more powerful impact on family dynamics.

This may also be at the root of the question as to why relationships between mothers-in-law and daughters-in-law are experienced as potentially more fraught than those with sons-in-law. Terri Apter[2] conducted a large-scale study interviewing both generations: mothers, mothers-in-law, daughters-in-law and sons-in-law. All of them locate the potential for emotional heat in the relationship between the two in-law women. Often daughters-in-law and mothers-in-law seem to feel that each other's communications leave them in a constant double bind with misunderstandings ruling the day on many occasions. If the relationship was reported to be negative, then 75% of those negative ratings were given to mother-in-law/daughter-in-law relationships compared to only 15% to mother-in-law /son-in-law relationships. Triggers for conflict between the two women tended to focus on perceived mutual criticism and overlapping loyalties with either partner or parent.

This is of particular relevance as the following picture emerges in both Apter's research and my own interviews: if relations between son-in-law and parents-in-law are hostile or distant, this does not necessarily seem to influence the daughter's continuing contact with her own parents, whereas a hostile relationship between a daughter-in-law and her husband's parents will have a powerful impact.

Daughters and their parents often continue relating to each other even if the son-in-law stays at a distance, without this being seen as a particular problem by either party. The same behaviour is not seen as acceptable for a daughter-in-law. There were several instances in my interviews when a mother described her son-in-law as easy and her relationship with him as good, when in fact she seemed to rarely see him and most of the time met up with her daughter and perhaps her grandchildren without him. In contrast, sons came more rarely on their own and daughters-in-law tended to be more often part of the gatherings. What struck me was that mothers were rather surprised when I pointed out that their "easy"

---

2   Apter, Terri (2009): What do you want for me? Learning to get along with In-Laws. London

sons-in-law seemed to be so by virtue of absence, whereas the expectations for the daughters-in-law were higher and the thoughts about the quality of the relationship more based on the reality of mixing together more often.

> Tina who had described her son-in-law as much easier than her daughter-in-law declares herself surprised: *"You are right, he is rarely there when I see my daughter and the children, whereas my son always comes with the whole family (including my daughter-in-law)."*

In other words, daughters-in-law are judged differently from sons-in-law. A crucial factor here seems to be the level of expectations: female to female relationships tend to operate along lines of greater self-disclosure and emotional intimacy. As described above, it tends to be women who maintain the task of intergenerational "kin-keeping" in families and failure to do so on the daughter-in-law's part is experienced as rejecting and hurtful. In my interviews the bar was a lot lower for sons-in-law: as long as they did right by their wife and did not prevent the relationship between mother and daughter continuing, there did not seem to be that much more that was required from them in order for the relationship to be judged unproblematic or successful. Sons-in-law were allowed a much greater degree of social and emotional distance. Expectations of the daughter-in-law are much higher. A daughter-in-law keeping the same distance is experienced as rejecting and cold, partly because rules of female interaction ask for higher levels of "intimacy" to be judged successful, and because the younger woman's attitude is experienced as having an impact on the older woman's relationship with her son. The power is seen by the mothers to lie with the younger woman who will decide how much relational work she is prepared to take on board concerning her own relationship with her mother-in-law, but also concerning the mother-in-law's relationship with her adult son and later her grandchildren.

Apter points out that girls engage from an early age in what she calls "borderwork", meaning interactions that decide who is in or out of groups and involving a high degree of scanning and interpreting of sometimes disguised meanings of communications. They are also more likely than boys to have practised this kind of borderwork with their parents, actively drawing and redrawing boundaries especially with their own mothers. Mothers and daughters alike report higher incidence, frequency and length of arguments with each other during adolescence than mothers of sons, thereby practising developing distances and acknowledging changing identities. Girls are after all under a different kind of pressure to negotiate where they stand as far as being like or unlike their mothers is concerned. Boys are different by definition. Girls are as a result more likely to have learned how to draw boundaries whilst maintaining relationships. What they have learned on the school playground, in friendship groups and at home leads to a high degree of sensitivity in women towards undertones of communications that often elude their male spouses who may be at times unaware of the silent or disguised war raging between their spouse and their own mother. Men often leave the borderwork to their wives and both mother-in-law and daughter-in-law have to carry this weight. Daughters-in-law and mothers-in-law often feel abandoned to the conflict by their male partners who may refuse to take a stand or even understand what it is that is happening between the two women. This in turn may encourage a process of projection where anger and disappointment with the male partner who is seen to be failing is in turn projected onto the other woman.

Relationships between mothers-in-law and sons-in-law are also often less problematic, because the daughter takes responsibility for smoothing away conflicts, whereas in the mother-in-law/daughter-in-law relationship nobody mediates on behalf of either party to the same extent. Sons can mediate in cases of conflict, but mothers-in-law are restrained in their room for manoeuvre by the powerful dictum of non-interference, described by all the mothers

I was talking to. The risk of conflict is also described as much more intimidating for mothers-in-law of daughters-in-law, as it is feared that open conflict could be more damaging and the relationship may not survive. This is expressed only to a much lesser degree by mothers of daughters.

Gransnet, an internet forum for grandmothers, is witness to all this. Posts concerning the relationship with the daughter-in-law far outweigh those regarding the son-in-law. A special section, AIBU (Am I being unreasonable?), covers many uncertainties regarding the reasonableness of mothers' own behaviour, and that of their sons, daughters and daughters-in-law, but sons-in-law rarely figure. Mothers' anxiety about getting it right with the female newcomer to the family far outweighs anxiety about the male newcomer, mainly because the power of the female newcomer to disrupt, maintain or even strengthen the mother's relationship with her adult son is judged to be much greater and the risk attached is assessed accordingly. The assumption that open conflict cannot be risked or successfully managed unfortunately seems to lead to simmering resentment and grievances. The prime anxiety of mothers that comes across loud and clear in these posts is the fear of loss. What is feared is the loss of closeness and intimacy with one's own child and the increased marginalisation that can come with that. It drives mothers into either aggrieved self-justifications ("All I did was... AIBU?") or troubled self-examinations and cautious tiptoeing. This latter strategy is something that had been practised anyway by many of them in the years of their child's early adulthood and continues from there to include any newcomers to the family. A repeated scenario described on the forum is one where the mother just thinks she has offered an opinion, but the daughter-in-law has interpreted this as attempting to interfere. This after all is familiar territory to any mother of an adult child long before in-law children appear on the scene!

It is important to keep in mind that while there can be very fraught relationships especially between mothers-in-law and daughters-in-law, when it works, the relationship between the two women can become highly rewarding. When daughters-in-law were loved by their mothers-in-law, they were loved in a deeper and more passionate way than sons-in-law. This also seems to be the case from the younger woman's point of view. This becomes particularly visible when the relationship between a woman's son and his partner breaks down, as described in the next chapter.

Entries and exits

Mothers are on the receiving end of their adult children's choices of partners. Whether the relationship between *themselves* and the son-in-law or daughter-in-law works out or not is of obvious consequence to them, however if the relationship between their child and the in-law newcomer turns sour, different issues arise.

Watching your child in an unhappy relationship can be very distressing. What comes up in conversation with mothers of adult children over and over again as a cause for distress is having to stand by while your child is in a relationship that is observed and judged to be unhappy, or even more than that, destructive or even abusive.

This can range from watching a child being unhappy in a way that may only be visible to the mother,

> Erica: *"I just know her too well and I can tell from the way she is always too busy to talk and always defensive, that something is not right and has not been right for a while."*

through observing the marriage of their child and feeling that the scales are tipped in favour of the in-law

> Monica *"His career is taking off, and she is just fading into the background. She says she is not interested any more in her own career and it is her choice, but why does she seem so irritable and unhappy?"*

to watching a child being trapped in an abusive marriage, whilst being helpless to do anything about it. The sense of powerlessness and distress is palpable in their comments.

> Teresa remembers: "*I had a lot of question marks from the beginning. He [son-in-law] had no friends, the relationship with his parents was non-existent. They decided to marry... what can you do? You have to give in. Now I'm just picking up clues. Things don't feel right. He tries to close her life down. I feel powerless to protect her and I'm just shelving my feelings when I am around him.*"

> Linda: "*I watch her [daughter] and the world she has created around her with him. It is not my job any more. And yet... how do you say: you are not happy, are you? You can't do that, not if you don't have a solution. It feels like walking through dark scary woods.*"

> Hanna: "*She [daughter] props up people who are needy and he [son-in-law] is one of them. He just behaves so selfishly and she does not seem to see it or mind. I actually said to her, come on, talk to me, I'm your mother. She knew I would be supportive of her, but she was not ready to see it back then.*"

> Emma: "*She [daughter-in-law] looks down on us and on him and it hurts seeing him being treated with so little respect. There is nothing you can do, it would just make things worse.*"

> Penny, whose daughter is married to someone Penny describes as a "*self-centred narcissist*", says: "*There is little you can do, you just have to go along with it and support them as best as you can. It's like walking on eggshells though. She knows me, she knows what I think even if I try to hide it.*"

> Susan talks of becoming rather "*mummy bearish*". "*I am not that sort of person generally, but anybody making them [her children] unhappy, is unfair to them: you become like that, even if it is entirely inappropriate... Of course there is nothing you can ultimately do, but be there.*"

The overriding emotion is the sense of powerlessness and feeling of being helpless as a bystander.

Short Story
Weight control

The early pictures had begun to arrive: as Sarah waited for her food at the café, she went through some of the photos on her phone, only casual snapshots at this stage, but in due course there would be more from the official photographer. The wedding had just been a couple of days ago, her daughter Kate, and Nick, her now son-in-law, would be on their honeymoon, and Sarah was trying to get back to some normality, coming back from planet wedding.

Her food arrived, but, rather than enjoying it, other images crept into her mind, images of her daughter Kate picking at food on her plate. Food should be nourishment, a joyful experience, to be shared with others, but then food can become so complicated. Kate seemed to increasingly just see it as calories, certainly lately that seemed to be the case. The wedding dress had been like a dreaded exam to her. The question seemed to be entirely whether Kate was going to be able to control her weight and her body sufficiently to fit the dress on the day. Like everything else about the wedding it had turned into a struggle to gain control, control of quite what became increasingly difficult to understand. Sarah did not seem to be able to get anything right for her daughter, who seemed to view her mother solely as somebody who might want to interfere in her wedding and had to be kept at arm's length at all cost. Sarah had been very anxious to show the right level of interest and excitement for her daughter's wedding, but she soon realised that she was between a rock and a hard place.

Too little excitement and she was seen to be too remote and not interested enough, too much and she was perceived as interfering. There was just no solution to this dilemma. She was certainly perfectly happy to take a back seat, so her daughter's constant suspicion that she was trying to interfere and take over her wedding rather puzzled Sarah. Kate's obsession with staying in control and fending off any outside interference did not stop with her mother though. Nothing about this wedding was going to be left to chance and her planning was meticulous and this extended, without any doubt, to her own body which had to be controlled in a variety of ways. It was as if her body became a project to be tackled methodically and the biggest challenge seemed to be her weight. Kate's body had to be controlled for this wedding it seemed, and whoever and whatever had to be fought in this particular battle, Sarah had somehow become part of it.

The pressure did not seem to come from Kate's husband-to-be. Nick was always very supportive of Kate, was repeatedly heard to say that he loved her just the way she was and he really did not care whether she lost weight for the wedding or any other time. He was a very sporty guy, a cyclist, very fit and very slim. In a strange symmetry Kate seemed to gain weight whilst he got fitter which had made Sarah uneasy in a way that she could not explain.

Kate had never been as slim as Sarah herself had been. Her daughter's body had stayed soft and rounded, but Kate had initially seemed to be happy in herself and did not yield to the food and body anxieties of her friendship group. How could she escape it entirely though? The problems were not even the images of airbrushed bodies, as unattainable as they were unreal, but the whole language that developed around food. Whether it was the language of diets, of allergies and food intolerances, of vegetarianism or veganism, of healthy food and unhealthy food, fattening food and food that gave you cancer, more and more food gained a near moral quality: good food and bad food, food you could proudly present as pure and superior and food that made you ashamed and marked you as inferior. Food marked your class, your sophistication or lack of it, your strength of character, your green credentials. Your body exposes it and there is no hiding. Mirror, mirror on the wall, who is superior amongst us all?

Actually it was more than a mirror looking back at you. It had to be posted out to the world: virtue signalling was one word for it, beauty signalling, success signalling, happiness signalling. Social media had not just Kate, but her whole generation, by the throat.

Could Sarah as her mother abdicate any responsibility for this though? Was it really all down to peer group and social media? How do you learn to love your body or, to the contrary, see it as an adversary? What protective layer had she failed to wrap around her daughter? What critical gaze may she have introduced? Sarah had certainly never intentionally made food or body size an issue with her daughter, but Kate had been caught up in it anyway. Sarah herself knew how to plan, to prepare, to organise, impose control. Her work as a PA in a large school demanded from her that she was able to create order out of chaos if necessary. She had standards, she was good at it, as she had been at organising family and work life when the children were young. It had not always made her popular, but people on the whole were relying on her and appreciated her competence. Kate had not always appreciated it. You would not expect that from your teenage daughter. Kate had had her own standards and these were quite demanding, *she expected a lot from others, her friends, her parents, but most of all from herself. Kate had resisted her mother's control and sometimes suspected control when there was none, but she had somewhere along the way started to turn the battle on herself. "Fight me," Sarah had often thought. "I'm your mother; that comes with the territory. Don't fight and punish yourself!" For what anyway?*

Those were the teenage years, but why had it again become such an issue now, with the teenage battles long behind them, when in fact Kate should have been at her happiest? Kate had after all found Nick, charming attractive Nick, and they both seemed to be devoted to each other. One thing that Sarah had learned over the years was that when her own relationship with her daughter became difficult, when Sarah did not seem to be able to do anything or say anything without irritating Kate, then there was often something quite problematic and separate going on in her daughter's life. As a mother she seemed to be repeatedly the lightning conductor for a distress that may not have been identified yet by mother or daughter alike. She just could not figure out quite what it was that caused Kate's distress in the build-up to her wedding to her perfect man.

Nick had tried to persuade Kate to join him exercising, particularly after she started complaining about gaining weight and generally losing motivation. They went running and cycling together, but of course he was much better than her and Sarah had noticed on occasions that his comments which no doubt were meant to be encouraging sounded rather patronising to her ears. Kate had got sucked into a cycle of giving up and trying again. Nick stayed calm, did not seem to judge, and yet: mirror, mirror on the wall? Nick was undoubtedly the fittest, the slimmest, even the calmest, the most encouraging of them all. He had control,

Kate did not. Sarah picked up her phone and looked at the photos of the wedding day again. Kate looked beautiful and happy. What nagged at Sarah was the impression that Kate seemed to be the one who thought she was the lucky one. Nick was clearly her great catch and she was the lucky one. How had that happened?

It was difficult to put your finger on it and at times Sarah had been struggling so much with the irritated hostility that her daughter seemed to direct at her, that she had little capacity for feeling protective and concerned. However, sometimes she sensed something when she was not even directly focusing on Kate. She found that she herself got more anxious about what to cook when Nick was at their house. He clearly knew so much about food and as a committed athlete cared about what he ate. He was always complimentary about what she cooked, but, knowing how he talked about food and other people's eating habits, she felt a slight anxiety creeping into her preparations. Just as she had felt odd about wearing a swimsuit in front of him on that family holiday in aid of her sixtieth birthday. Her younger daughter's partner had not bothered her in the slightest, but Nick had. Her problem? Her problem alone?

Talking about it with Kate was impossible. For a start all this may not really be relevant for Kate, and Sarah did not want to create an issue when she may well be just overreacting. There was also the fact that Kate was hypersensitive to anything that could be interpreted as a slight of Nick. Once Sarah had taken Nick on and attempted to make a bit of a joke regarding the holy grail of fitness – his fitness. Kate had actually laughed and clearly quite enjoyed the moment, but Sarah noticed that Nick was not at all amused. He had not liked them laughing together, harmless as the occasion was, just part of some family banter.

The next morning Kate had complained that Sarah had been attacking Nick and that Sarah did that often and that she was quite attacking of people in general. Sarah was completely taken by surprise and hurt by how quickly and suddenly Kate had turned on her and launched into this generalised personal attack. Yet she had also felt protective and concerned for her. Above all she knew she had to be careful. It had indeed been quite a while before Kate and Nick had visited again.

Sarah tried to wave away the thought clouds that had formed, as they suggested in the meditation app that she had used during the long year in the build up to the wedding. Should she worry? Would it help? She tried to focus on what was in front of her, her plate of food, the street scene that had delighted her only a couple of minutes ago, but all she found herself doing now was assessing people's looks, their body shapes, their clothes, judging, however hard she tried not to, knowing she herself would be judged too. What was it that had got into her the moment she thought of Kate, the moment she thought of Nick?

Later that evening she looked at more wedding photos that were now pouring in on her phone. There were also the first photos from the honeymoon. Kate had taken them, all of them of Nick of course, apart from the one selfie where she was a bit too close to the camera. Sarah stared at one photo that was taken after what must have been a hang-gliding adventure. "So proud of my wife," Nick had posted. The honeymoon they had chosen allowed them to engage in a string of physically demanding and challenging activities and the pictures told the story. Sarah had been particularly puzzled about her daughter's choice of honeymoon. Why would Kate want to do that? It was just so unlike her. Which was indeed the question: why did Kate want to do that? It wasn't as if Nick had forced her to do it, she had agreed, had declared herself excited about this new kind of venture. And now looked strained and anxious on her selfies...

There were other people in the hang-gliding group, young men looking very much like Nick and young women looking nothing like Kate. Perhaps this was a fantastic opportunity for Kate, getting out of her comfort zone, trying new things. Wouldn't you want that for your child? What did you know as a parent of an adult daughter about what was like her or not like her? It was unfortunate that the phrase "reshaping herself" popped up in her mind. Was Kate's constant battle to control her weight and reshape her body now intrinsically linked with pleasing a husband whose shape was becoming a benchmark? What if Nick was ever so subtly gaining control by encouraging Kate to stay locked in that battle?

What if it was? And, if so, what then? What could Sarah do? Was this the final frontier of maternal control?

As described in the above short story, mothers may feel helpless watching their child trapped in an unhappy or complicated relationship, observing but with nowhere to go with what they see.

However, they may feel equally helpless when their child's relationship with their partner does in the end actually break down.

The news of an adult child splitting up from their spouse or partner will impact considerably on mothers and mothers-in-law. Mothers may feel deep concern and distress about the situation their own child is in following a split or divorce, whether this concerns economic hardship or emotional distress. They may on the other hand feel confusion or even rage about the decision their child has made, if their child was in fact the driving partner in the separation. Mothers who are grandmothers may also feel enormous anxiety about their own access to grandchildren. This is particularly the case with mothers of sons where the daughter-in-law often has control over access to the grandchildren, and a continuing relationship between mother-in-law and daughter-in-law is crucial for the grandmother. Mothers tell of the efforts they are making to keep the connection with their grandchildren. I heard of one case where the son's mother concentrated on the relationship with her daughter-in-law's mother, the other grandmother, as relations with her daughter-in-law had just become too difficult. Most grandmothers seem to try to keep some link with their ex daughter-in-law, often out of genuine affection, even solidarity with her, but most of them admit to some tactical thinking. They also talk about having to keep a precarious balance: they try to keep in touch with the ex-daughter-in-law on the one hand, mainly to maintain easy access to the grandchildren. On the other hand they try to be seen as not taking sides, both for the sake of their relationship with their own child and beyond that for the sake of their relationship with their child's future partners. This is clearly not an easy feat, as emotions around separations of this kind are likely to be very raw for all participants.

At best mothers and mothers-in-law can provide a non-judgemental calm space, at worst their anxiety and taking sides will inflame an already difficult situation.

If the relationship between mother-in-law and son-in-law or daughter-in-law has been a good one and if in fact it may have reached a rewarding level of affection and intimacy, particularly between mother-in-law and daughter-in-law, then the news that there are difficulties between the mother's child and their spouse, that indeed the relationship is coming to an end, can be devastating for the mother-in-law. Mothers-in-law are not likely to be consulted about any decisions, but they will rather be informed about them and are expected to stay on their child's side, even if they are not necessarily happy with their child's behaviour. Either way, they find themselves in a situation where a significant loss is inflicted on them over which they have no control. Particularly if there are no grandchildren present, the general expectation is that the contact between them and their daughter-in-law or son-in-law ceases, often very suddenly and without much warning. They may feel that they are experiencing a genuine and substantial bereavement without really being acknowledged as mourners and having to hide their feelings.

> Jan: "*I knew his girlfriend as a girl when they were both very young. They travelled together, they were together all of the time. When they split up, I felt such a terrible grief, I had to keep very busy.*"

> Susanne talks about her daughter's ex-boyfriend: "*He was great, such a lovely, warm, fun person. Then it was suddenly over and you realise, that is just it. This person had just disappeared from my life. After that I decided I was not going to become emotionally attached to them again. I was not going to let anyone into my life when I had no control. I just can't let myself.*"

> Evelyn says: "*I still miss her, after all these years. She was so supportive of me when my son seemed to have very little space in his head for me. He made me feel I was unreasonable, but she stayed on my side and understood that those were just very hard years for me.* [Evelyn's partner had died.] *And now she is gone and I am just supposed to get on with it, as if my relationship with her had been completely irrelevant. He even said: it's my life, Mum, it's got nothing to do with you. Of course it's his life, but how can it have nothing to do with me? She was his wife, first and foremost, but to me she was also like a daughter, and I have lost her.*"

> Louise describes being on the receiving end of her sons' partner choices (divorces and remarriages) as "*rolling with the punches*" which sums up the situation rather neatly.

Whatever turn their child's relationship with their partner takes, mothers are on the receiving end and their feelings are something they feel they have to keep very much to themselves.

Monsters-in-law: cultural stereotypes

There is another dimension to becoming a mother-in-law that will influence women's experience even if they are not necessarily directly aware of it. Family relationships after all take place not just in the confines of our private and individual circumstances, but they happen in a historical and cultural context. We cannot experience and perform these relationships without being influenced one way or the other by what we know our roles to be and what cultural expectations are associated with them. We may want to avoid following those expectations or perhaps try to fulfil them. We may think they have nothing to do with us, and yet they are likely to provide a powerful frame of reference. In Western societies, particularly those of a Northern European or Anglo-American flavour, the emphasis on separation and independence as markers of successful adulthood creates a different framework of expectations than is present in societies where family ties have an overriding importance: in such societies expectations of how successful adulthood and successful family extensions through marriage and grandparent-hood are managed will look different. Family, so sociologists tell us, is after all what we take it to be. It is a construct that tells us who we regard as "family" and what we see as our obligations towards them and bonds with them. Culturally influenced definitions of family vary and with them expectations of how for example adult children are supposed to relate to their families of origin and their in-laws. As heard in some of the interviews, in Mediterranean societies for example, it may well be seen as the norm that adult children before they get married still live with their parents. The same scenario in northern European cultures is seen as the exception that needs an explanation, such as economic needs. Talking about "my family" may well lead to different expectations of whom the speaker is referring, the extended family or the nuclear family, depending upon which culture the speaker originates from. Family members being there for one another means different things, depending on whether you assume you are talking about the nuclear family or the "clan", creating potentially substantial differences regarding support for the elderly or support for the generation bringing up children. It also shapes the reality and expectations of mothers' position in their adult children's lives.

The power of cultural expectations and associations becomes particularly visible around the role of the mother-in-law. Mothers-in-law do not get a good press. The stereotypical mother-in-law displays characteristics such as interfering, controlling, bossy, possessive, jealous etc. This stereotype will inform the perception of all participants. It may lead to anxiety and attempts to avoid such a fate on the one hand, and on the other hand it can lead to fitting observations of real interactions into a particular schema and giving them a particular interpretative tilt. As such it has real power to shape the experience that family members have of each other.

The negative stereotype of mothers-in-law runs through different cultures. It is present in fairy tales and myths, in literature, film and media. A study by Parnell[3] explores examples ranging from literature in ancient Rome through African contemporary TV series, from Japanese films to European fairy tales, modern children's films, British horror films and American sitcoms: the stories all resemble each other in that they depict the older woman as a controlling, dangerous and competitive presence who tries to control her children. At best the mother-in-law may appear as a kind of killjoy keeper of tradition, overprotective of her own children, at worst as a dangerous and overpowering figure trying to control her children's decisions and meddle and interfere in their lives and relationships. In European fairy tales it is often the stepmother rather than the mother-in-law who fills this role. It is interesting to note that the terms themselves overlap, the English

3 Parnell, Jo (2018) Representations of the mother-in-law in literature, film, drama and television. Washington and London

term stepmother being interchangeable with mother-in-law until the middle of the nineteenth century. In French both mother-in-law and stepmother are called "bonne mere". The characteristics are the same: they are women who are interlopers to a family unit, legal mothers only, attempting to take the place of the biological "good" mother, who has disappeared, having died before the story starts. They embody the opposite qualities to the "good" mother who is supposed to be nurturing, protecting and selfless, the "bad" legal mother embodying the opposite qualities of being selfish, manipulative and possessive. They are trying to control their stepdaughter or daughter-in-law and their own child with destructive and – in fairy tales – at times murderous intention. They may attempt to steal their children, as does the witch in Rapunzel, or to destroy their chance of good fortune and love as do the stepmothers in Cinderella and Snow White. They create dark domestic environments, often trying to use their destructive power when the biological parent (the king/father as in Cinderella) or the young male protagonist, their son or an intruder who wants to marry into the family (as the prince in Rapunzel) and who may have offered protection, are absent. In the end the innocence and power of the wronged younger woman is established, love invariably triumphs and the mother-in-law/stepmother is punished. The level of violence in the punishment is often disturbing and some fairy tales have since been edited to make them more acceptable as children's stories.[4]

One reason for the dominance of this negative image may be the fact that originally in most rural patriarchal societies the new wife would have joined her husband's family and the mother-in-law's role would have been to socialise her daughter-in-law into her new family's customs and way of life, as is still the case in some societies. This gives the older woman considerable power. The

---

4   Diller, Luisa (2008): The complete book of mothers-in-law. London

potential abuse of this power is still a horrifying reality for some women.[5]

Increasingly however this power depends on the mother maintaining her bond with her son, creating a potential rivalry with the new spouse. With the modern shift from hierarchical family relationships, with their emphasis on respect and obedience between children and parents, towards an emphasis on horizontal relationships of affection between husband and wife, the older woman's position becomes weaker. In literature and modern media representations she is increasingly depicted as an irritating but pathetic figure. Her attempts to gain or maintain power are always portrayed as negative. If she was originally the "bad" mother who is at war with her daughter-in-law, she can also in modern tales, such as in post-war British horror films (see for example: "Fanatic" and "Persecution") and American sitcoms, become the emasculating mother who has raised weak sons and troubled children and is still interfering in her adult children's lives. The mothers and mothers-in-law who cannot let their sons go are often portrayed as not only being an obstacle to their sons becoming adults and forming independent adult attachments, but beyond that as having raised weak, emasculated and often dangerous men ("Psycho"). Younger women and daughters-in-law in this scenario disturb the unnatural attachment between mother and son and become therefore a source of conflict. Inevitably our loyalty as readers and viewers is drawn to the younger woman claiming a natural order of generational succession in this battle.

In Western society multi-generational households are becoming rarer and, as a result, the presence of mothers-in-law in their children's lives is reduced. The power base has undoubtedly shifted. Some of the surviving negative associations around mothers-in-law

---

5   Geetangali Gangoli (2013): Violence between female in-laws in India. Journal for international women's studies. Vol 14 , p147-160

may tap into an existing anger at repressive and interfering parents, but I think beyond that they tap into a wider misogyny and a particular fear and hatred of old age and older women in particular. Old men in fairy tales become wizards displaying wisdom and grace; old women become witches, physically repulsive and full of evil intent! Men can be told not to behave like "an old woman", there is no equivalent stereotypic expression as in behaving "like an old man" that could be levelled at a woman. As an insult, "prick" or "dick" does not carry the same venom as the c*** word. The level of personal nastiness displayed in reactions to older female politicians (eg Teresa May, Hilary Clinton), and older females in public life in general (eg Mary Beard) far outweighs the level of nastiness that is on the whole directed at older men.

This quality is particularly noticeable in mother-in-law jokes, present since music hall days, and songs and burlesques since the late nineteenth century. Again the ubiquitous nature of these jokes about mothers-in-l"aw stands in stark contrast to the absence of jokes about fathers-in-law. The mother-in-law is always depicted as a harridan, a belligerent female, interfering and possessive.

> *"It's obvious she doesn't like me – she calls me effeminate. I don't mind, because compared to her I am.*
>
> *I saw six men kicking and punching my mother-in-law. My wife said: aren't you going to help? I said, no six should be enough."*
>
> *"Why would you rather deal with a vicious dog than your mother -in-law?" "A vicious dog eventually lets go."*
>
> *"How many mothers-in-law does it take to change a lightbulb?" "One. She just holds it up and waits for the world to revolve around her."*
>
> *"Two men were in a pub. One says to his mate 'my mother-in-law is an angel.' His friend replies, 'you're lucky, mine is still alive'"*

And so on...

Given the fact that, as discussed above, in *reality* tensions are more likely to exist in the mother-in-law/daughter-in-law relationship, it is interesting to note that mother-in-law jokes are without exception told from the son-in-law perspective, locating resentment and hatred of the mother-in-law in the son-in-law. What is happening here?

When looking at visual depictions of mothers-in-law which accompany some of these jokes, for example on seaside postcards, they often show her as an imposing masculine figure, bigger in size than her son-in-law.[6] On stage she is often played by male actors and the Les Dawson gags create a kind of uber masculinity suggesting the potential of the mother-in-law to undermine the son-in-law's masculinity and male authority in his own household. Mother-in-law jokes demonstrate male fear and hatred of powerful maternal figures and they have at the same time a distinct controlling function. After all, the butt of the male jokes may be the mother-in-law, but the trigger is nearly always a suggestion that the wife may be under her mother's influence and therefore be more difficult to control by her husband. Whilst the jokes claim to be picking up issues of boundary transgressions committed by mothers-in-law, they in fact ridicule and discredit the private lives and modes of relating between female members of a family system. Mother-in-law jokes are thus used to regulate both wives and mothers-in-law: stereotypes influence perceptions and create behavioural taboos for women in both generations leading to regulation and self-regulation: being powerful is to be avoided at all costs, for older women, for mothers-in-law and for women in general. Ignoring this taboo puts women at risk of hatred, attack and ridicule, and they know it.

---

6 See Parnell, Jo (2013): Representations of the mother-in-law in literature, film, drama and television

Psychological angle: mothers and mothers-in-law

Where does this fear and hatred of older women originate? Why is it so powerful, both in the external perception of older women and in their perception of themselves?

"Nothing quite ages you as much as your child growing up", as one of my mothers wryly observed. What she means of course is that your child growing up *confronts* you with the fact that you are growing older, it brings home what is happening anyway and interrupts denial which otherwise may have been maintained for longer. This can be a both liberating and painful process.

We do live in a culture obsessed with youth. Ours is not a world where "elders" are valued or wisdom of age is commonly referred to. There is no general interest in the experience of older people; they are more commonly ignored, often dismissed and declared irrelevant. To declare yourself "old" holds no positive associations, to look or feel old is seen and experienced as a kind of failure. This can find material expression in the increasing array of physical transformations through pharmaceutical, cosmetic and surgical interventions in which women are invited to take part, a never ending "anti-ageing" campaign. The binary view of young and old separates attractive young bodies and faces from their antithesis, old bodies, faces and minds which in turn provoke fear and revulsion. The maxim is "not to let yourself go", encouraging an increasingly fraught battle with the process of ageing. The older person reminds the young where they too are heading, and the young person's fear leads to increasing manoeuvres of denial. The older person has to be "othered", kept away from any position of relevance in the young person's life. Any demonstration of power and competence in the older person, particularly the older woman, can threaten this denial and disturb the younger person's view of themselves as being firmly on the other side of the divide of youth and ageing. General cultural and individual misogyny merging with fear and hatred of old age make older women the target of resentment and abuse in a more powerful way than men.

What interests me for the purpose of this book is the question of how being a mother of an adult child forces women to enter this battlefield, both in how they are perceived by others, but at least as much in how they perceive themselves. It may be out of an individual woman's awareness, but deep down women, and in particular older women, know that they have to be careful or risk becoming trapped in hostile stereotypes. One of the consequences seems to be that mothers report high levels of anxiety about being perceived as interfering, bossy, opinionated. As a result they engage in a high level of self-monitoring and attempts to restrain themselves, staying in the position adopted when their child reached adolescence, namely anxious tiptoeing. This has partly to do with the appropriate realisation that they need to "step back" and respect their child's adult independence. However, there is an extra dimension to this that has its roots in the knowledge that, as older women and mothers-in-law, women face a certain amount of culturally determined hostility. They may indeed have a highly complicated relationship with themselves as women who are now growing older, agreeing to some degree with these stereotypes and fighting their own getting older, as has been highlighted for them by the adult status of their child.

Whatever a woman's attitude to herself, with a child growing up comes the realisation that it is now another generation's "turn", a realisation that becomes particularly visible at certain milestones in the adult child's development: maybe their first "proper" job, the first purchase of a house, or a wedding in all its symbolic significance as previously described, certainly with the arrival of a first grandchild. It is now the child's or the young couple's turn and the mother is increasingly in the position of the observer of her child's life and relationship with another, rather than a participant. Generational succession involves acknowledging that the focus of action between the generations has shifted to the younger generation. This involves many joyful experiences, yet also demands an acknowledgement of one's own ageing.

An interesting perspective on this is provided by the psychoanalytic view of this stage of parenthood which is seen to retrigger old conflicts along the lines of what psychoanalysts describe as the early oedipal conflict. The oedipal conflict in psychoanalytic thinking describes the child being confronted with the realisation that his/her mother and father have their own relationship that the child is not part of. Whilst the child has his own dyadic relationship with mother and father, he/she has to come to realise that he/she is also a witness to the parents' relationship with each other from which he/she is excluded. Working through this realisation and the accompanying feelings of jealousy and exclusion, envy and mourning, is seen as a crucial part of healthy development. Any situation in adult life which resembles this original childhood one can trigger unresolved conflicts of this phase and everything that has been learned in connection with it. The relevance of this for parenting of adult children when they settle with their own partners seems clear to me: to increasingly become a witness to, rather than a participant in our children's life and relationships is after all one of the greatest challenges for mothers, as already identified. Whether we can accept as mothers that this is now where we are in our relationship with our children and their partners without raging against it, without trying to fight it or collapse into depressive reactions, will determine how we experience this stage of motherhood. We will need to work through our own feelings of mourning the passing of our own youth, and the envy that may be triggered seeing the new generation taking their turn. We have to come to terms with our new relationship with our child in which we are less central: a true developmental challenge. Its success will depend to a great degree on how able we are to face those difficult feelings and this in turn will tap into coping strategies which have been developed a long time ago in a person's history. If we can do this in an honest way, we can find a creative response to the changes that we are experiencing. (See chapter 4 on individual case studies for further detail.)

What to do and how to be

How to be a good mother-in-law? A vexed question...

- It seems to me to be crucial to give up on that time-honoured maternal habit of feeling we are responsible for everything and, if in doubt, to be blamed for all things going wrong. When our children bring their partners into our families, the field gets more populated and more complicated. These newcomers bring with them their own personalities, family histories, their expectations and intentions. Whether we get on and how we get on with them is not entirely up to us. That may be a problem, but it can also absolve us from having to carry the enormous burden of having to make this work single-handedly: we can't, however hard we try! So accepting that may be a first step.

- Don't believe all the success stories around you. Not getting on with your son-in-law or daughter-in-law or generally finding it hard work adjusting to the new situation is something that many of us are ashamed of, and may see as a personal failure. As a result, mothers do not necessarily talk about it and instead present their families as successful and unproblematic. Don't feel a failure comparing yourself to such success stories.

- Accept that you are going to be increasingly more of a witness than a participant. This is the way it has to be and fighting it will not help. Again, accepting change rather than seeing it as something that can be resisted will help both your perception of it and your behaviour towards the next generation. In fact, your relationship with your child and their partner is likely to be less troubled as a result, and ironically a greater degree of participation down the line, maybe as a grandmother, may be on offer.

- Be curious, be interested in the newcomers. Particularly for mothers-in-law of daughters-in-law it can be an enormously helpful and indeed rewarding experience to get to know each other as independent women rather than just in your family roles. You are both women with an overlap of experience. If you can see her less as a rival but more as another woman, she may respond in kind.

- Know yourself! If you are aware of your vulnerabilities and how they express themselves, you can be more prepared for thorny territory and perhaps guard against overreactions. Is your daughter-in-law really that competitive or are you very sensitive regarding a perceived danger of being pushed out? Is, for example, being excluded or ignored something that figured highly in your family of origin? Keep it separate as much as you can. More on that in chapter 4.

Chapter 3

Becoming a grandmother

Many of my interviewees had already welcomed or were about to welcome another group of newcomers into their family: they had become or were hoping to become grandmothers. Without exception this was regarded as a highly significant life event that signalled a major shift in family dynamics. The prospect of involvement with grandchildren was welcomed by a high proportion of my interviewees and many of them seemed to be overjoyed at the news of the impending arrival of a grandchild. In fact some of them seemed to have eagerly and impatiently waited for this news. In many interviews I was taken back to the impression I got in the interviews I did for *A Wedding in the Family*, namely that many women had nurtured this fantasy for quite a while: a young woman may imagine and even plan her wedding without any particular man being part of the plot, she may dream of having children and even have names for her unborn babies. Older mothers may in a similar way fantasise about their adult child's wedding day and indeed the grandchildren that they hope they will have one day. Mothers admitted to keeping their children's toys "for the grandchildren" long before there was any likelihood of a grandchild arriving. Cots were kept in lofts, and there was many a tale of mothers being more or less subtle in telling their children that maybe it was time to "make me a grandmother". Often I was told about this with a laugh, but there was no doubt that many mothers felt not just concerned for their child, hoping that they would not miss out on this experience of parenthood, but also concerned for themselves, wishing to be part of this stage of the family life cycle.

Not all my mothers however had necessarily been overjoyed at the news of the forthcoming arrival of a grandchild. They may have felt that their child was not ready for parenthood or that they were not in the right relationship or that financial circumstances were not right. They may also find that they themselves are not ready for grandmother-hood. "I don't/didn't feel ready to be a grandmother" was a sentence I heard a lot. Often this is mirrored in the thinking about what they might wish to be called:

> Bryony talks of not expecting the grandchildren to call her "grandma". "*That's not what I feel like.*" Later she adds, "*Being grandma is a very different thing from one person to another, I have not found out yet what it is.*"

> Tina asks: "*How to be a grandmother? I'm a visiting grannie... that is unchartered territory. What will she call me?*"

Sometimes the unease in the anticipation of grandmother-hood refers to an anticipation of the practical involvement that may be demanded, when the woman in question may wish to have time for herself and her own often postponed goals and projects. In reality this fear is matched by the fact that many grandmothers do indeed take on a significant proportion of active childcare. Particularly in families who live within closer proximity to each other, grandmothers do not just "help" with childcare, but they "are" the childcare, regularly looking after grandchildren for often several days a week. This seems to be a generational shift and many of the mothers in the interviews commented on the fact that they would not have dreamt of asking their mothers for the same support. The shift is partly due to increasing numbers of young families with both parents going out to work and partly to the forbidding costs of childcare. In the UK, grandparents and grandmothers in particular form an army of unpaid labour looking after grandchildren full time or part time. According to the gov.uk website grandparents provide the main childcare for 35% of families where the mother is working and they tend to provide around ten hours a week on average. This saves parents approximately £6.8 billion nationally in childcare costs. The report states:

> "Although most grandparents enjoy caring for grandchildren, those who provide care for longer hours are less satisfied and more likely to report a negative impact on their health and wellbeing."

The increasingly delayed age of mothers having their children means that the average grandparental age has risen in parallel. This may make looking after grandchildren physically more demanding, but at least these older grandparents will not necessarily be financially disadvantaged by providing childcare. Younger grandmothers may have to give up work in order to help with childcare, with implications for their current financial situation and their future pensions. Many of the younger grandmothers are also sandwiched between care for their grandchildren and care for their own parents, which can put a halt to any ambitions they may have had for time for themselves. The importance of grandparental childcare became painfully visible during the recent pandemic when the advice for older people to stop physical contact with their families left many young families without the childcare they needed to go to work. The creation of "support bubbles" may have been presented as a measure to lessen the pain of separation and loneliness, but it certainly was also answering the growing need to get parents back into a position where they could work.

The slight unease expressed by some of my interviewees was also linked to a distinct perception that grandmother-hood ushers in old age associated with grey hair, knitting and a kind of benign, doddery irrelevance. The fear of losing one's identity that often accompanies becoming a mother for the first time seemed to make a reappearance at this stage of becoming a grandmother for the first time. Just like before, the fear seemed to be that becoming a grandmother would somehow put a stop to a woman's non-domestic and non-family identity. Being again sucked into a very female nurturing and domestic role was not always felt to be an attractive prospect.

Whichever camp the women I interviewed fell in, once they had grandchildren, they described, without exception, being a grandmother as a joyful experience, often also one that initiated a shift in their relationship with their child.

> Bryony, whose daughter is expecting her first child cautiously comments, "*I have friends who are grandmothers who assure me it is wonderful.*"

> Paula recalls that when it happens: "*All of a sudden all that love comes in.*"

> Rani calls her grandchildren "*a gift, a joy, we love them to pieces.*"

> Alejandra describes being a grandmother as "*one of the best experiences of my life.*"

> Paula enjoys the fact that her granddaughter "*is my biggest fan, it lifts up my life.*"

> Susan says: "*I just love holding them, being with them. They take care of us, holding our hands. To see her [daughter] with them, it is quite amazing.*"

Susan's last comments echo what many mothers described. It is not just the grandchildren, but the experience of seeing your own child being a parent can be intensely moving. Particularly mothers of daughters describe the confusing sensations of seeing their daughter pregnant, with memories of their own pregnancy rushing back. As in the very early stages of motherhood, here again I was told of the slight confusion of body boundaries, seeing "my baby having a baby" as Mary put it, which puts mothers in touch with the sheer physicality of pregnancy, childbirth and early days of looking after a baby. Then, increasingly, it is about watching the adult child growing into becoming a parent. If they do so successfully, mothers describe intense joy and pride.

Gemma about her daughter: "*She just took to it like a duck to water.*"

Sally about her son: "*I had no idea he could be so gentle, the way he holds that baby.*"

Jenny: "*They are brilliant parents.*"

These are just some of the comments I heard from proud grandmothers, proud of their children as well as their grandchildren.

Mothers also describe that they notice a shift in their relationship with their child. This may be due to the adult child's change in perspective when looking at their own parent, maybe the beginning of a new appreciation of how complicated being a parent can be and with it a new tolerance towards one's own parents. Maybe the shared experience of loving this new arrival in the family creates a new bond. From the grandmother's point of view the child's becoming a parent seals in a way the long journey from child to adult and what has been an ongoing process often comes to a point of full acceptance at this stage. Mothers of daughters and sons alike often comment on a new closeness and a softening of their relationship.

Erica: "*She [daughter] clearly appreciates me more, she actually says thank you and clearly means it. That does not sound like that much, but we have had years of me not getting it right, so it is a huge shift.*"

Grace: "*We were all sitting together in the evening and he was holding the baby, and then he [her son] looked at me, and it was such an open look, he had this big feeling and he could share it with me.*"

Livia: *"After my granddaughter's arrival my son was back asking for advice. I had a role again."*

Having a grandchild can be a second chance: a second chance to bond with your adult child, but also a second chance of being with a small child and all the potential delights, of physical proximity, of undiluted love. The difference is that this time round most grandmothers do not have the burden of responsibility and pressure to run a busy life at the same time. "The beauty of it is, you can hand them back" is a refrain that I heard over and over again. Grandmothers often provided long days of childcare, some travelled long distances to do so; they covered long school holiday periods and were certainly at times feeling rather stretched by this. Even those grandmothers who were regularly involved in childcare and at times felt rather exhausted by it commented that they were still able to hand the child back to the parent at the end of the day and what a big difference that made. They felt that they could devote themselves to the grandchildren in a different way than they had been able to do with their own children at the same age, when they had to run busy lives concurrently. For some this was like a second chance, heightened by an awareness of how fast these early years go by.

Short Story
Gratitude

The old woman sat with the baby and through the open kitchen door she could see the planes circling in the dark summer evening sky. There was a soft hum of traffic, a faint glow of London's lights, but otherwise all was quiet. The baby had finally gone to sleep. His head rested on her chest, his warm body moulded itself against her, and she could feel his little belly moving, softly and rhythmically, like a bee. This is it, she thought, there is nothing else, this is all there is.

She had told her daughter-in-law to go to bed, she would look after him until he needed another feed. Liliana had not protested: she looked translucent with tiredness, her mass of dark curly hair nearly overpowering her pale face, her soft body looking vulnerable and frail. She had smiled and said "Thank you", and the old woman had felt flooded with love and gratitude towards this young woman whose child was now her grandchild, whose husband was her son.

The baby was shifting his weight and sighing and she froze, not to disturb him. "Like your daddy," she whispered to him, "like I sat with your daddy." Your daddy, who is now a tall and quite imposing man (how did that happen?) who wears suits and has a grown-up job (how did that happen?), who as a little boy used to rush into her arms in sheer delight (where did that go?). Just seeing him had made her fill up with love, filling her up to the brim. Now, more often than not, he is a friendly stranger and the old woman could not really see the line between the baby she used to sit with and this friendly stranger.

She had worked throughout his childhood, there had never been any question about that, so had her husband. Her mother-in-law had provided most of the childcare and the boys had been looked after well. She had always worked, even as a child. At school she had been one of those girls who teachers could rely on, working hard and achieving, not shying away from responsibilities. She had been well trained: her mother's unhappiness and the break-up of her parents' marriage had seen to that. She stayed at home when her mother could not get out of bed, became her mother's confidante and carer, inventing excuses for school, and making up for it with extra work, so that nobody would ask questions. That was just the way it was. The playfulness of her friends' childhood was alien to her, theirs a foreign language hinting at a world she could only just imagine. She could not wait to get away, but moving away from home had proved not to be enough. Her mother's demands for her attention did not diminish and she found herself speaking to her mother daily on the phone, always feeling she would somehow be punished for her selfishness and for leaving her mother behind. Eventually she got married and had found herself without real surprise in a new family whose work ethic kept her in the same iron grip, but at the same time provided a protective layer against her mother's demands. She had not been unhappy, the boys had grown up, both of them settled in successful careers, a credit to her, as everybody said.

The baby started stirring and the old woman started rocking her body gently and rhythmically. A cat moved towards the open kitchen door, watched the woman rocking herself and the baby, then turned away to continue to explore the night in the back gardens of the big city.

She had not been unhappy with her life; she had not had any expectations that could have been disappointed. She had just never really been a young woman with the lightness and hope that she imagined would have come with that. When the boys had grown up and left home, that had been a bit strange at first. She had found their lives strange, though she liked the fact that people seemed to think that somehow their lives were proof that she had done her job as a parent well. Her younger son had married and settled abroad, near his wife's family, but rang regularly enough and they never failed to remember birthdays and special occasions. Her older son lived not too far away, but that did not lead to much more contact either. It was always nice to see him, though she really did not know much about him any more. And alongside that she had turned into the old woman she now was, slightly bewildered at the life lived so far.

When he had brought Liliana home, it had been like a sudden burst of colour into the perfectly pleasant grey of her life. From the beginning she had radiated warmth, openness and goodwill towards her mother-in-law and the old woman had felt herself melting. Her own family did not really hug, but Liliana seemed to want to touch people all of the time, including the old woman who was not used to touch any more. She would link arms when they were walking, touch her on the shoulder when showing her something. More than that, her son too seemed to soften. He and Liliana seemed to be always touching each other, but never in a way that made you feel uncomfortable and excluded, rather in a way that made you want to smile with them. He started hugging her when he came to visit, the boy who had rushed towards her emerging like an early version of a painting hidden behind later versions. It was if the young woman had found her son and brought him back to her.

And now the baby. When Liliana became pregnant, the old woman had feared that she would be put back into her box. She had seen other women's sons getting married, other women's grandchildren visiting. In the village she had lived in all these years she had seen it often enough, long visits to the family of the daughter-in-law, popping in briefly to the family of the son. That was what she had prepared herself for. She had left her mother and now her boys would leave her, a just punishment. When her younger son moved abroad, she found she had trained herself to live with that for most of her life.

Liliana and her family however seemed to want to share, to include. She had met Liliana's mother before the wedding when she had come over from Spain to help her daughter choose a wedding dress. The old woman had not expected to be invited, but Liliana and her mother had insisted. When Liliana stepped out of the changing room in the wedding dress, she had felt like crying at the beauty of it, but at the same time felt this was a bit ridiculous and it was not really for her to cry, she was not the mother. Then Liliana's mother had taken the old woman's hand and squeezed it tight, including her in this moment and giving her the right to cry. In his wedding speech Liliana's father had thanked them with what seemed real feeling for looking after his daughter. During the ceremony Liliana's mother had taken the old woman's hand again and this time she had squeezed it back, letting herself sink into the generous embrace this other family offered.

When Liliana got pregnant, she must have missed having her mother around, and the old woman tried to look after her as best she could. Sitting next to this young woman who carried her son's child, who would happily lead her hand onto her belly: "Feel, feel, it's kicking!" The movement of the baby inside the young woman's body and her memory of her son moving inside her had merged in those moments, her daughter-in-law's delight and generosity over-layering some tighter, tenser quality of the memory.

The baby was getting restless and it would soon be time for his feed. She took in his smell, the slight dampness of his face against her skin. "That is the beauty of being a grandmother," her friends had said. "You can hand them back". They had not told her that something would be handed back to her, but this time it was lighter and warmer and younger.

> *She took the baby into the bedroom, gently waking her daughter-in-law. Liliana smiled at the baby and at her mother-in-law. "Thank you," she said again. The old woman smiled too. "Thank you," she replied.*

Becoming a grandmother was however not always a smooth and rewarding process for some of my interviewees. A lot of the mothers I spoke with acknowledged that the attachment they formed with their grandchildren made them more vulnerable, as if the safety distance that they may have developed during the years of their children becoming increasingly independent had been disturbed. With the arrival of grandchildren the on/off-ness of the closeness and interrelatedness of mother and adult child has now reached a stage of potentially heightened "on-ness". Contact tends to increase or is expected to increase at this stage of the family's life. When that does not happen, this is felt to be painful. Geographical distance that may have been tolerated well enough becomes a different challenge: Face-timing with your grown-up son in Australia is one thing, attempting to be a grandmother across such a distance is a completely different challenge. There were mothers in my interview group whose children had decided to move away, sometimes abroad, after the grandmothers had already bonded with grandchildren who had become a hugely important part of their life. The pain and grief resulting from such separations were palpable. Others had foreseen this development when their child settled far away, but were still overcome by the raw pain of trying to figure out how to be a "remote" grandmother. It is interesting that some of my interviews were conducted during the pandemic with its lockdowns and contact restrictions. All of a sudden most grandparents found themselves in this same situation, and there was no doubt that this was the most distressing aspect of the pandemic for them. They scrambled to fill the gap, stories being read online, webcams being set up in children's rooms, activities being designed that could be done over the internet. The younger the grandchild, the bigger the challenge. The most distressing aspect seemed to be that not only would they never get this time back, but also that they feared it would not be possible to establish or maintain a meaningful connection with the grandchildren. Grandmothers missed the physicality of the interaction with a small child, but they also feared that they would lose again what they had lost before with their own child and had found again with their grandchild: the uncomplicated, easy love, not marred yet by the necessary disillusionment and complicated nature of loving a grown-up "child".

Grandmothers' bond with their grandchildren also made them at times more vulnerable in another way. One mother described it as being a "hostage" from now on. Losing the grandchildren or indeed their love would be a significant blow and it could happen in different ways. The most harmless way is the natural progression of time and grandchildren growing up. Many grandmothers who were a bit further down the line with older grandchildren were aware of the fact that it was not always very easy to keep the connection. Teenagers being more interested in their devices than direct contact with grandparents was interestingly one of the most mentioned issues, followed by teenagers being more interested in peer contact.

> Grace has an example of this: *"They are just forever fiddling with their phones and Grannie just does not hold the same allure anymore... So now when I come and visit, I don't see that much of them anymore."*

Others expressed a feeling of being at times rather taken for granted by their child or being reduced to being a provider of childcare:

> Michelle: *"I am only on my son's radar as somebody who babysits."*

Tina: "*I have been called on a great deal and they take it for granted.*"

A slightly sinister dimension was added by the observation that the very fact that grandmothers bonded with their grandchildren made them more vulnerable to what some of my interviewees openly called blackmail.

Paula suspects: "*She [daughter] does not like me to be close to the grandchildren. She doesn't do sharing, one wrong move and there will be sanctions.*"

The idea of "sanctions" as something that can be imposed as punishment and which could take the form of reduced contact with the grandchildren was very present in some of my interviews. In the most serious cases there was substantial estrangement between grandmothers and their grandchildren. This may be the result of a divorce and the son-in-law, or more often the daughter-in-law, being in control of and hostile to contact. It may be the result of an estrangement between grandparents and their adult child. There are numerous posts on *Gransnet* about that kind of estrangement and the pain and bewilderment is very clear. What comes across most powerfully is the sense of total lack of control and the helplessness the women feel in this situation. It is worth stating that I have no way of telling why the adult children of these women have chosen to reduce or withhold contact from their mothers. All I am focusing on here is the mothers' experience. Grandmothers who have been estranged from their child and thereby their grandchildren will in these posts almost inevitably talk about not understanding what happened. Often they blame the child-in-law and, more often than not, the daughter-in-law. Some may acknowledge that they played a part in it by not being diplomatic enough. Often there is a history of a difficult relationship with their own adult child in question. Whichever way, the pain that is caused by this estrangement leaps off the page. One of the longest posts I have seen which ran over many pages, deals with the question of how to "not let estrangement ruin your life", as most mothers in that situation admit to hardly being able to think of anything else. In the posts that deal with merely difficult relationships the possibility of this eventually leading to estrangements is ever present. As one of my interviewees put it:

"*They [the adult children] hold all the cards.*"

Advice given by members of the *Gransnet* forums always suggests stepping back, not offering any advice unless asked for, or, as one poster put it:

"*Keep your mouth shut and wear beige.*"

This last curious bit of advice struck me as quite interesting. Without a doubt, women have to adjust to their position as observers and supporters of the core family rather than being inside the core family unit: this is something that has been the central task for years of adjusting to being a mother of an adult child. "Keeping your mouth shut" means understanding that these are your grandchildren and not your children, this is your child's marriage, your child's life and not your own. This has never been clearer than when grandchildren arrive, and grandmothers who have done their emotional work on stepping back will be better prepared for this. On the other hand there is the "wear beige" aspect of it that links back to women's ambivalent feelings to becoming a grandmother: my interviewees had expressed anxieties about this potentially being a challenge to the non-family, non-domestic identity that they may have forged for themselves after their children had left home. Some of them had developed decidedly non-beige lives and felt that this new identity suited them. There was a sense that this had to be re-negotiated yet again, together with the boundaries between themselves and their child's family and their child's life.

In my interviews it became clear that this was by no means an easy process and feelings of frustration lay close to the surface.

Susan says: "*I know my place.*"

Marian observes: "*They all read the same books, they all think you have no knowledge or experience. It is very frustrating. I have just given up now. I don't make waves, my main purpose is to maintain the relationship with the grandchildren. I just keep quiet really.*"

Lauren states: "*We do it the way they want it not the way we want it.*"

"*It's better to keep your mouth shut. It's ok to know things, you don't have to tell people.*".

Gail: "*We mentioned it, but we were firmly told... I felt very shut out.*"

Irene: "*I have to let it go. If it was my child, I would be in there.*"

Anna: "*If you look on* Gransnet *there are hundreds of people not seeing their grandchildren. I settle for quite a low baseline, for what I can get, not what I expected.*"

Samira: "*My daughter-in-law is a bit harsh with the children, but I cannot say anything.*"

These are just some of the comments indicating the struggle these mothers are experiencing. Some of them have clarified in their mind their new position.

Erica: "*We are part of the extended family, not part of their core family.*"

Eleanor: "*This is his baby rather than my grandchild.*"

Jayne: "*My primary role is not to be a grandparent to my grandchildren, but to be a parent to my children, to teach them how to be parents.*"

Tricia: *"There is little you can do, it's best to support them."*

Even grandmothers who have adjusted to their new position can feel the effort and pain of this adjustment, some more than others:

Tricia is identifying clearly what she feels: *"Letting go, standing back, it is like an ongoing bereavement."*

Another mother expresses in this context a feeling that she has been surprised by:

Vicky: *"I wouldn't admit this to people, but really deep down the baby is another rival."*

This last comment especially serves again as a reminder that the maternal journey towards a satisfactory relationship with an adult child involves the capacity to become part of a new triangular relationship, to stand aside and observe and tolerate another relationship rather than being a central part of it. This involves the ability to tolerate feeling left out. The arrival of a grandchild emphasises this. This new baby is not the grandmother's child, she is not the one who knows best or who can make the decisions regarding his/her wellbeing. She is definitely also having to let another person, the new grandchild, take up centre stage in her child's life.

As discussed in the previous chapter, psychoanalytic thinking suggests that the grandmother's capacity to tolerate this situation will be grounded in her own history and how she learned to survive what psychoanalysts call the oedipal conflict.[7] This refers to a

---

7 Wrottesley, Catriona (2017): Does Oedipus never die? In: Couple and Family Psychoanalysis. Vol 7, no 2

child's first attempts to accept that he has to share his mother's love and attention with another, as the mother has relationships that are independent from him/her and to which the child is just an observer: mother's relationships with her partner, with another baby, with her friends, etc. In other words the child may or may not develop the capacity to tolerate triangular relationships. If things go well, then it becomes possible to be both outsider and insider at the same time, to share and to enjoy observing another relationship without feeling overwhelmed by the threat of exclusion. A grandmother's own experience at this early age will have a profound effect on her capacity to witness a relationship later in life, as she has to do now again when becoming a grandmother. If things have gone wrong for her at this very early stage of her own life and if she has not successfully learned how to creatively enter into this position of witnessing a relationship, then the arrival of a grandchild is going to be a more serious challenge for her than for women who have a more solid base for tolerating being an observer rather than a participant.

All grandmothers will have to find their own way of dealing with the realisation that, not only are they observers to another relationship, but that it is now clearly the next generation's turn to have procreative relationships that are no longer available to the grandmother. All grandmothers will have to deal with the fact that this emphasises the fact of their own ageing and the need to hand over the torch to the next generation. Some find this too difficult to tolerate and engage in some form of manic denial. Competitive behaviour of various shapes can be the result: insisting on youthful "I am not a grannie" behaviours can express this just as much as treating the grandchild as if it was their own baby. Here we can then see the grandmothers who "help" by attempting to take over the care of the baby, who enter into some rivalry with their daughters or daughters-in-law for the child's affection, for knowing best and being the expert. Often one can observe confusion over generational boundaries, when for example grandmother and mother seem to form the main "parental couple", or grandmother and son seem to form the core unit, with the daughter-in-law being given a bystander position. The grandmother/mother couple are probably the most common "couple" as the experience of pregnancy and childbirth shared by mother and daughter can form a strong connection between the two women, and grand-maternal experience may make her the most likely go to in cases of anxiety and need for reassurance and support. In some families, particularly maternal grandmothers are very hands-on in the first months and even years, providing a substantial amount of the childcare. However there is a fine line between giving support and taking over, and if that goes wrong, then fathers and grandfathers may well feel side-lined in such situations. In a couple of my interviews I had difficulties establishing whether there was indeed a father or whether the daughter was a single mother, as the father was not mentioned by the grandmother at all. To some extent this seems to be generally experienced as more acceptable than the "couple" forming of mother and son with the resulting side-lining of the daughter-in-law, the mother of the baby. When the paternal side of a family is dominant, or where the separation between mother and son has still not been successfully established, this can set the scene for long- lasting power struggles between grandmother and daughter-in-law, and indeed to serious trouble between the young couple, particularly if the husband is not supporting his wife's position sufficiently.

Grandmothers who have managed to internally negotiate how to be an observer rather than a central participant seem to find more helpful solutions and embrace the position of witness in a more joyful way. The mothers in the interviews who could enjoy seeing their children become parents are examples of this. It is from this position that they can give their children the support that they need, moving on to let their children form the next generation and supporting them in that move.

The grandmother's challenge to observe another relationship rather than to be a core part of it is tested in an additional way that I have not yet mentioned: this is not her baby, but her child's baby. She is not the mother, but the grandmother. More than that though, she is not the only grandmother. Her child's in-law family who may not have figured much after the wedding, if there was one, are now becoming more visible. After all, there are likely to be at least two sets of grandparents, maybe more due to separations and subsequent marriages, all of them with the same "right" to be grandparents. The struggle to adjust to this is often a strong feature of emotional reactions to weddings, when the two families have to figure out how to welcome a newcomer to their family but also how to see their child join another family with its inevitable territorial struggles. This is all being reactivated with the arrival of grandchildren. The "battle of the grannies" is well documented in *Gransnet* posts. Grandmothers being anxious about being pushed out of the family by the "other" grandmother is a repeatedly discussed topic. There may be just a neutral statement like:

Bryony: *"The other grandmother is part of the care set-up."*

There may be a slightly humorous hint:

Meriel: *"We are not rivals in any way, and yet the competitive aspect is undeniable. We all want to be the favourite grandma."*

There may also be more agonised descriptions:

Debora: *"She [the other grandmother] picks them up from school most days, we just visit a couple of times a year. We are the occasional visitors, we don't really stand a chance."*

Fiona: *"They [other grandparents] have all that space, when they come to us it is all cramped and everybody gets irritable."*

Christine: "*She [daughter-in-law] takes them to her parents every week, but they never bother to pop in here. The children don't even know I live in the same town as their other grannie.*"

Charlotte: "*I will be the 'other grannie'.*"

Gloria: "*He [grandson] said to me the other day: you are not my real grannie, Grannie S is my real grannie. He doesn't know what he is saying, but it hurts.*"

Anne: "*My presents just disappear, but theirs are on constant display.*"

Very often territorial questions have literally to do with territory, the young family living nearer one sets of parents than the other. Often the question becomes one of what one set of grandparents can provide in terms of time, money and entertainment. Sometimes the link with one family is stronger due to the effort made by the young couple. Problems can develop if the link is not well maintained by the mother's own child, or even sabotaged or neglected by the child-in-law who looks after the connection with her or his own family more. However much the grandmother in question may be aware of the fact that the grandchild will benefit from strong connections with many adults, including several grandparents, anxieties about being left behind or excluded can often make this quite difficult.

The more secure the grandmother is in her connection with her own adult child, the more relaxed and generous she can be as far as her grandchild's attachments are concerned.

Megan: "*The more people there are who love the children the better.*"

What is very clear is that on the whole we are talking about a lengthy adjustment process: just as becoming a mother is not only a question of giving birth but in fact a process of developing over time a new identity and learning a new way of relating, so is becoming a grandmother. The arrival of a grandchild marks only the beginning of a journey during which all central relationships are being reassessed and rewritten: we become grandmothers by learning how to relate to our grandchildren, but, more than that, we become grandmothers by learning how to change our way of relating to our own children as parents. This is a process that will have been ongoing for some time, but will now have a particular creative poignancy.

what to do and how to be

- Step in: your child becoming a parent means that they need you in a new way. Providing care for an infant is such an enormously steep learning curve. It is not just full of physical and practical challenges, but it is beset with enormous anxieties, uncertainties and emotional upheavals. Young parents need all the support they can get and who is better placed to provide it than the people who care deeply for them and for the new arrival. This may be the time where you have to reset priorities for a while and give what you can give. The reward is the changing relationship with your child and the growing relationship with your grandchild.

- Step back: this is not your baby, it is your grandchild and you are in the second row of support, not the first one. You may well know better, have more experience, observe your child "making mistakes". It is not for you to decide what is right or what is wrong. It is the next generation's turn to figure out how to parent their children and you are a witness to that, a supportive witness, but not a core participant.

- Your child holds the baby, you "hold" your child. The better you can figure out how to do that, the better your child's chances of being a good parent. Tell them how well they are doing, build up their confidence, listen to their anxieties. Give them breaks to catch their breath.

- Enjoy your grandchildren. You are old enough to know how fast time moves. Don't miss it. Allow them to slow you down in a way that you probably could not afford to do with your own children. You will give them something different to what their parents can give them and they will give you something that you can savour and must savour.

Chapter 4

Like mother like daughter

W hen I interviewed Stella, it was shortly before Christmas. As in most families with adult children all over the country Christmas arrangements were being discussed. Where were their adult children going to spend Christmas? How were they dividing their time between their family of origin and the family of their partner?

I heard mothers repeatedly describe a pattern that seemed acceptable to them: the adult child comes home for Christmas, even if they have lived away from the parental home for a while. If they have settled with a partner, there may be years of both young adults spending time apart from each other at Christmas, going back to their family of origin. This is often followed, maybe after a wedding or the arrival of grandchildren, by years of the young couple spending Christmas together, but dividing their time between the two (or of course sometimes three or four) families, often alternating one Christmas at one family, the next with the other family. Eventually the role of hosting Christmas may shift over to the younger generation. The logistics can be fiendishly complicated, particularly when there are more than two families involved, due to divorce and remarriage. However, on the whole most mothers could agree quite easily on the rules which symbolically provide a map for the negotiation of family relationships with adult children, once their new partners are part of the picture.

Such unwritten rules become visible when they are broken: in Stella's case she was struggling with the fact that, again, her son's fiancée had refused Stella's invitation to come for Christmas and was spending Christmas at her mother's. This Stella could have accepted easily. What proved more complicated was that, again, her son was expected to join his fiancée's family. The rule of taking turns was broken and Stella was not surprisingly concerned about much more than Christmas. Was this going to be the future alignment of the families? Soon it became clear though that there was yet another dimension to her distress. She spoke about her own Christmas celebrations during the early years of her marriage and how this had worked out between her family and her family-in-law. Almost as an aside, she mentioned her father's second marriage and how she had always felt she was treated like an afterthought at Christmas by her stepmother who had clearly put her own children first. Stella's father had not stood up for her then, and nor did her son now.

What this story highlights is the fact that few things truly happen to us for the first time. Our mind seeks patterns, compares and filters new experiences through past experiences. Often our emotional reaction to events makes a lot more sense when we take this into account. Stella is upset about her son's decision, but the hurt she feels is also informed by past experiences, maybe outside of her direct awareness, but powerfully influencing what she feels nevertheless. Her son is not the first significant man who puts her second.

In my interviews with mothers this showed up over and over again. Whether stepping back is easy or excruciatingly painful, whether jealousy is manageable or not, whether abandonment lurks around the corner of any rejection, these are often the results of past experiences shaped in an equally intimate family context, that of the family of origin. Mothers of adult children have not only been mothers of small children in the past, but they have been daughters before and their mothers have been daughters before them.

Short story
Christmas Eve

It stood for "Darling Husband"; she figured it out in the end. "DH" stood for "Darling Husband" and MiL stood for mother-in-law, DiL for daughter-in-law. Once you got that, it became easier, though some expressions still puzzled her. She had discovered Gransnet, an internet platform for grandmothers, and she scrolled through today's posts again, a lot of them "wondering whether I should speak up", a lot of them "heartbroken", "estranged from children and grandchildren". Well, she was not estranged from her son and his family. In fact, they were coming soon to stay with her for Christmas. She had certainly been happy when she was able to tell friends about it. What are you going to do for Christmas? My son Tom and his family are coming home. Perfect, that had definitely been the answer that was required.

Janice was scrolling through the posts on Gransnet. "Nannyfaraway" felt disrespected and misunderstood, "juno12" agrees being a grandmother is so hard. Hostile DiLs, neglectful children, "but you have to let them go, you know".

She had let him go, in fact it had been less difficult than she had expected, even though he was her only child. Maybe because he was her only child, she had been so aware that she must not smother him, hold on to him, and it had actually been a nearly naughty pleasure letting him live his independent interesting adult life and meeting up with him occasionally, adult to adult, having breakfast in a café, a drink in the evening, going for a meal. He would tell her about his life and she would tell him about hers and feel so grateful that this was how it could be. She had not really suspected that this too was just a phase.

He would meet up with his father too of course. There had been a couple of difficult years after the divorce, but everything had become a lot easier after that.

She looked at the Christmas card that Tom had sent. It was a photo of him, Mandy and the children. A photo in black and white, looking both arty and playful. Mandy was pulling the sledge, Tom and the children were sitting on it. Mandy looked strong, attractive and radiant, Tom had that charming little boy smile which he was beginning to look too old for. As she so often did, she looked at the images of the children, Noah and Miriam, scanning them for family similarities.

When Noah was born, her first grandchild, that was what she had done straight away. They had sent her a photo, taken soon after his birth. She had hoped for a little boy, but when she looked at the photo, she realised she had hoped for a little baby boy like Tom, looking like Tom. Instead, Noah had Mandy's colours, her mouth, and Janice had felt that Noah had been offered to her and yet a little distance had been introduced at the same time. She had kept looking at him in the following months, years, hoping for something that visually linked him to her son, to herself, and of course in the end she just saw him as Noah. She had never forgotten that strange disappointment in the first moment.

They would be here soon. She had offered to pick them up from the airport, but they had insisted they get their own hire car. This of course would give them their independence and they were likely to want to visit friends when they were over here. She did not really mind, in fact she knew that having a break from the children would also be quite nice. She was not used to the energy and noise of small children. She would be able to joke with her friends about that after all, join them in their proud tales of chaos, "you know what it is like". In fact she was not sure that she knew what it was like for them or that they knew what it was like for her.

Closing down the Gransnet posts she looked around the kitchen. She was prepared, Christmas decorations, Christmas food, presents, all the time keeping in mind whether Tom might like some of the old Christmas of his childhood and how much of it would be what Mandy and the children wanted. She had to guess, with Mandy you often had to guess. She did not give much away as a rule. She was never rude or unpleasant, but there was a distinct absence of making the slightest effort to please that Janice found surprisingly unnerving. She herself had always tried to please her mother-in-law certainly. It had not been difficult, her mother-in-law had seemed very happy with her and they had stayed in contact after the divorce. It had been important to achieve this, to be liked and to be approved of. Sometimes she was surprised herself, how important that seemed to be, just as it was now important to be liked and approved of by Mandy and she had been, of course, prepared to work hard to achieve this. Mandy however did not seem to feel the need to make any particular effort. She was just polite, pleasant and supremely uninterested.

Janice had regretted never having a daughter, although she could see that friends with daughters did not always find it as rewarding as one might have expected. Particularly after the divorce, she had been in awe of the power and beauty of female friendships, the intimacy, the solidarity, the loyalty, the fun. It puzzled her how so many of her wonderful friends seemed to have such complicated relationships with their daughters, it seemed to come with the territory. She had wondered though what it would have been like to have a daughter herself, and later she had wondered what it may be like to have a daughter-in-law. Could there be friendship or something close to it? Fun? Solidarity? If Mandy was capable of any of these, and after all she did have girlfriends and her relationship with her mother seemed close, there was certainly nothing offered to Janice. Just an absence.

She resisted the temptation to look for further posts on Gransnet and went through her to-do list. The whole complicated choreography of a family Christmas... When Tom was little, she had been exhausted by the marathon of pre-Christmas school activities, present lists, food preparations, getting the house ready whilst work created ridiculous deadlines. Her parents would have arrived a couple of days early to help, always seeming to be slightly intimidated by her life, her house, her husband, her in-laws who would come over for some part of Christmas. They certainly had tried to please, tried not to get in the way, tried to be helpful and tried not to irritate their son-in-law. In fact their constant trying had irritated Tina beyond belief. It still made her feel guilty, how she had wished her parents had had her parents-in-laws' easy charm. They never needed to try. They just owned it.

She wished she knew what Tom and Mandy's plans were. There was always the question of when they would leave to join Mandy's family. It was of course her turn this year, but it did not always work out like that. She had actually been tempted in the past to create a spreadsheet to show how much time Tom and Mandy spent with her and how much time they spent with Mandy's family; how petty. Mandy's parents were charming people, so were Mandy's two sisters, married with children, cousins for Noah and Miriam. That was so nice for the children, so lovely, everybody so bloody charming and lovely. The force of her anger took her by *surprise and nearly winded her. Not now, wrong timing, they would be here soon and she had to be relaxed, welcoming.*

Where was the list? Even if nobody else really cared, she would feel better if she had everything prepared, if the house looked nice and Christmassy. In a bizarre way it felt like she was doing this for the house, rather than anybody else. As if she could still keep the house blissfully unaware of how things had changed, still believing it was providing the magic that worked when nobody was in fact that bothered anymore. The house has got dementia, she thought, it has forgotten the last few rather unsatisfactory and painful Christmases, but is happily stuck in the long term memory of happier times. It still thinks it can excite its guest, whereas I am under no illusion. Again the anger! Where is the list? There must be things to do.

This anger was becoming a problem, she knew that. Initially she had tried to be reasonable, to check out whether she was overreacting, whether she had misunderstood something, misinterpreted something. Often of course she had. But the anger was just waiting there; it waited for her to let it in and increasingly it just let itself in. That was certainly the end of any remnants of charm and loveliness. What is that they read out in church at Christmas? "Let us pray for the lonely and the unloved." What about the angry ones?

Gransnet had an abbreviation for it: AIBU, or Am I Being Unreasonable. All these women and their rage. Their rage and their anxiety that somehow they may have got it wrong. All these stories full of grievances, disbelief, bewildered hurt. They all told one story, a story of women without power, losing power, maybe never having had it in the first place. At least that is how they all seemed to feel: why does my daughter not come to see me anymore? Why do they withhold the grandchildren? My son-in-law is a bully. I seem to say the wrong thing all the time. What have I done? Is this normal? On and on it goes...

Had she ever have power? There were certainly times when she did not even ask the question. She was successful at work, her marriage seemed good at the time, and her son... Well, of course she had had the power, she was his mother, but that is not how she remembered it. What she remembered more than anything is how easy life had felt when Tom had loved her as his mother, the way a small child can love his mother. She had always felt a bit irritated with dog owners and their need for a pet that showed this peculiar limitless devotion to its owner. But there was something in a small child's love that was not that dissimilar. She had seen it in her son's eyes: that she was lovely and beautiful and good and worthy of limitless devotion. You don't get that for long periods in life: if you are lucky you get it as a child from an adoring parent, later from a lover maybe, and then from your child for a limited period of time. There had been no anger during those periods, she had liked herself, liked what they had mirrored back to her.

Her parents had both since died, her husband had left and her son... well, he certainly mirrored back something much more complicated now. Often she could not read him, often she had to guess, with him too, not just with Mandy. She saw herself in that mirror and it was more difficult to like that image: an old woman, often irritating, demanding even, trying but failing. She wasn't even sure that she knew what exactly she was failing at. She wasn't sure whether he saw the rage. She wasn't even sure whether she made it all up: AIBU?

She put the to-do list away and opened a couple of recent Christmas cards. They were from ex-students, thanking her for what she had done for them, her encouragement, her example, her ability to motivate. She had been good at her job as head of department, she was quite sure of that. She had been a good teacher and a good colleague, fair, co-operative and generous. Would Tom describe her like that? Unlikely, and Mandy would not be interested either way. In an unguarded moment Tom had admitted to her that Mandy did not regard Janice and Tom as a proper family, not as proper as her own, with Mum and Dad still together, siblings, nephews and nieces, the whole glorious Christmas postcard family. She was just a fragment of a failed family to Mandy, maybe deserving a bit of pity, mostly just to be ignored. She had no power: there was the anger again.

Had Mandy ever tried? Had Janice somehow missed the point when bonding between her and her soon to be daughter-in-law could have happened? It was not as if there was any visible conflict or jealousy. There had been no rows, no scenes, just this polite disinterest. She clearly just did not matter particularly to Mandy, and Tom did not seem to mind. He seemed happy with her, which of course was what mattered most. Why, if they were happy, did they have so little to spare for her?

Mandy would send WhatsApp photos of the children but not engage in a text conversation, and although she always thanked her for birthday presents for the children, they never seemed to be visible when she visited. She wasn't sure what was worse, to feel the rejection or to feel so very petty in even noticing these things.

When Tom and Mandy had announced they were going to get married she had been aware that she had probably not been excited enough. She thought this was because weddings just didn't do it for her, but maybe she would have been excited had Tom been marrying someone other than

Mandy? The preparations for the wedding had unfolded and she had hardly been involved. In fact Tom seemed to be hardly involved. The ceremony was to be held in a field, no marquee even, a "wellies and brollies" wedding as it was called on the wedding website. Of course there was an enormous amount of planning going on, though Janice did not hear about the details unless Tom came to her for a moan. In the end during the last couple of days it was all hands on deck, and she had finally been allowed to help. Everybody had worked flat out and she had felt included at last. It had turned into a lovely day in the end though and she had felt pleased with herself, as if she had behaved well and passed the test. In the warm afterglow of the wedding she had expected some kind of acknowledgement, a reward for good behaviour, but it had not come. She had not figured much in the photos and when they talked about the wedding afterwards, none of the anecdotes referred to her, it was as if she had been a guest amongst many others. She had sold the rather expensive hat that she had bought for the day on eBay; it had felt it was almost mocking her, this marker of her status of mother of the groom. MoG on Gransnet?

When Tom and Mandy had announced that Noah was on the way, that had felt like a second chance. They would be a family, she would be their child's grandmother: it had to be a second chance. It had become clear very soon however that she was one of two grandmothers and definitely the second in line. The starring role had been reserved for Mandy's mum. Curiously it did not look as if Mandy's mum had really been applying for this part. She already had grandchildren; some of them already lived quite close to her, whereas Mandy and Tom were going to live abroad. It was not a rivalry set up by the two grandmothers, but rather it seemed that Mandy's chance had come to re-claim her mother, to present her with a grandchild as her sisters had done before her. She was going to have her mother to herself this time, Mandy was going to be in favour and back in the nest. There was no time for another grandmother in this. Of course Mandy's mother had seen and held Noah first, of course she had stayed with them to help Mandy. Janice could easily understand and accept this. Mandy needed her mother in a way that Tom did not need her in his transition to becoming a father. There had been Noah of course, lovely little Noah, and the bond between them had been such a marvellous joy. The relationship between her and Tom and certainly her and Mandy had however not changed a great deal. If anything, conversations had been less personal, there was very little time and what there was would be filled with activities with the children, particularly after Miriam had been born and family life became the chaotic busy affair it should be. She had felt a bit of an afterthought, an attachment, not particularly necessary for proceedings, and Tom had just been so busy, coping well with the demands of fatherhood. She had been proud of him, happy to see him devoted to his children. If only there had been a bit more of a closeness between her and him, the odd confirmation of a still existing special bond, if only she had felt more included. Maybe she was, well, being unreasonable? Expecting too much?

It was beginning to get dark now. She switched on some of the Christmas lights and it did after all put her into a festive mood. This was the best hour, everything was done, her bit was done, and in the quiet she could look forward to them coming, her grandchildren's excited voices, their warm little bodies, their delight at seeing her still to come, still a possibility. A silent night, a quiet time with its memories

> *of childhood, her own, her child's, and now also with its possibilities. Hope for something to be given to her again.*
>   *Her phone buzzed: they were on their way from the airport. They would soon be here.*

This short story alludes to the subtle links between past and present. Janice's feelings regarding her relationship with her parents, her parents-in-law and now with her daughter-in-law, all display different variations on a similar theme, namely that of the need to please and find approval and the sense that other people hold all the power.

I shall draw on a couple of examples from my interviews to illustrate this point further.

There was one comparison concerning present and past that was mentioned by many women, namely whether they saw a similarity between their adult child and their own parents.

"She is like my mother" or "he is like my father/brother" are phrases that I heard a lot, particularly with reference to "difficult" daughters and sons resembling difficult figures in their mother's past. And this not surprisingly influenced the way the relationship with the adult child was experienced.

Maggie

Maggie, for example, describes her own mother as cold, narcissistic and utterly self-centred. When Maggie's daughter Megan enters adolescence and early adulthood, Maggie finds this very disturbing. What somebody else may view as fairly typical adolescent behaviour, namely self-absorbance and a distant and disinterested attitude towards her mother, Maggie sees as evidence that her daughter is finally doing what Maggie had suspected for a while, that is turning into Maggie's mother. Throughout Megan's childhood Maggie has found it difficult to focus on her daughter's needs, to deal with the self-centredness of childhood, not because she cannot see that a child might well be entitled to a certain amount of self-centredness, but because it opens too many wounds of having to tend to another's needs, in her case her mother's needs, at a time when this should not have been Maggie's concern, ie when Maggie herself was a child. Now with Megan becoming an adult, Maggie feels doomed to be stuck again in a relationship over which she has no control and where her dislike for the other person is palpable: to her own distress she dislikes her daughter because "she is like my mother". What makes this harder is that Maggie always felt her own relationship with her mother was difficult due to her own failings and shortcomings. "There must be something wrong with me" was what she believed. In fact just being a girl was clearly a mistake, as her mother remarked to the midwife when Maggie was born and chose to repeatedly repeat in public as if this was a particularly funny story: "if it's a girl, you can have her". Maggie confesses she herself would have preferred a "naughty little" boy to a daughter. Now here she is, stuck in another mother/daughter relationship which she feels is bound to go wrong, and again this is surely going to be her fault. When her daughter tells her that she has been seeing a psychotherapist who apparently told her that her mother was never there for her, Maggie is distraught: "She won't talk about it. I am not given a chance to understand it". Either way, Maggie is inclined to take on the responsibility, it must have been her failing.

Sharon

Sharon also talks about a distant mother. Hers was an upbringing in boarding schools, visiting her parents who lived in a different country, the geographical distance mirroring an emotional distance that forced Sharon into a self-sufficiency and premature independence that still shows now. Her delivery is unemotional and any attempt I might make to draw her out of herself is met with slight surprise and alarm. Her current family follows the family pattern of geographical distance. All her children have settled abroad, her daughter on a different continent. Visiting her involves a long-haul flight of an intimidating duration. Sharon's pattern of visits creates a rhythm of either having intense contact with her daughter and her grandchildren or none at all. How does she cope? "It's like going to the dentist, you just have to do it". She is aware that her age means that these journeys will not be possible forever. "Going there every year, but for how long? You protect yourself by not thinking too much that one day you will not be able to go. I am amazed I can do that." Listening to her, I am less amazed: after all coping with the contrast between close contact and none at all, the repeated change-overs from one life to another, were part and parcel of her childhood. Sharon was trained well for the life she is leading now.

Paula

Paula's mother suffered from schizophrenia and Paula spent her childhood in fear of her mother and her unpredictable states of mind. She felt her mother was cold and she can sense the same coldness in her daughter. "Sometimes I am afraid of my daughter the same way I am afraid of my mother". There seem to be some real mental health issues and the daughter's partner choices and addictive behaviour suggest that Paula is not inventing these parallels. However, her reaction and helplessness is heightened by the sense of "not again!" This, she knows, can lead to overreaction and misinterpretations and she is trying hard to learn "not to expect too much". She is feeling "very isolated, very afraid". Just like with her mother she is aware of the possibility of "sanctions" in reaction to "wrong behaviour" and she is on guard all of the time. She feels her daughter "can read me, she can see what I think". A lot of mothers of course comment on the fact that their daughters can read them only too well in spite of trying to hide thoughts or opinions. In Paula's account this has a different quality though, and the experience of living with a schizophrenic mother and being exposed to her internal chaos without another adult making things safe for her shines through when she talks of her fear to me.

What struck me in my conversations with mothers is that such parallels, happy and unhappy, are sometimes quite outside of the mothers' awareness and show up in their stories only when you know how to look for them. Some mothers name them directly, like Emma, who tells me of her warm and tolerant relationship with her mother-in-law and professes that she takes her lessons in her dealings with her daughter-in-law from memories of that past successful relationship.

> "I am not sure how to be a mother-in-law to my son-in-law, but I feel very surefooted in my relationship with my daughter-in-law. My mother-in-law taught me how to do it well."

Or Gina, who has had a loving relationship with her by now deceased mother which seems to have weathered the changes throughout their lives well.

> "Your relationship has to change, it makes it easier if you accept that and my mother was very good at adapting to our different situations. She was always there for me, but in changing ways, and she had her own life, so I had to adjust to her changing too. There was just a steady core of being really important to each other and knowing we would be there for each other. That has taught me a lot about how to be with my own children. It makes me less afraid of change."

Doreen struggles with her relationship with her daughter-in-law.

> "*She is somebody else's daughter. She is very close to her own family and I have to accept that.*" Later in the conversation she refers to her own mother-in-law, saying, "*My husband has a much closer relationship with my parents than I have with his mother. She is just not an important person in my life.*" Clearly she expects this pattern to be repeated now with her daughter-in-law: "*That is just what we know.*"

Other mothers seem to be quite unaware how much the past weighs on the present and how it can feed anxieties, resentments and reactions.

Carole

Carole, for example, is struggling with her relationship with her daughter and has found in particular her daughter's settling down with her new husband a real challenge. She is constantly afraid that her son-in-law's family will be closer to the couple and that she will be for ever "in the second row". Her daughter's behaviour seems at times very distant and often outright hostile, but it is not entirely clear to me how much Carole's anxiety contributes to this, over-interpreting events or indeed maybe provoking them. What clearly makes things worse is that Carole knows mother/daughter relationships can fail, as did her own with her mother.

> "I sometimes see she [daughter] look at me and that look scares me. When she was a teenager, she would look at me that way, but now that look is back and maybe it will stay. I remember looking at my mother like that..."

When Carole was a child, her father died and her mother remarried. Soon afterwards her twin step-brothers were born and Carole was sent to boarding school. Throughout her childhood she struggled with the sense of being an outsider and having to be "good" to be included. Her relationship with her mother was dominated by her own resentment and at the same time the need to please her. So now, when there are new rivals on the scene, in this case her daughter's husband and his family, she can see that it is indeed possible that she may lose out. "They" can send you away and you will only be able to see the new happy family from afar, the outsider looking in.

Viv

Another example of this is Viv, whom I interviewed when her son was about to get married. We were sitting in the living room of her town house overlooking the park. The room was furnished with antique and modern furniture, clearly carefully chosen. There was a piano in the corner, the walls were lined with books, and there were beautiful objects displayed throughout: the room felt like an oasis of taste and cultured serenity. Viv seemed to be enjoying the interview, talking about the forthcoming wedding with an air of amused detachment. Her son, a professional musician, was marrying a young woman whose family had embraced the wedding preparations with some enthusiasm. It was going to be a traditional big wedding dominated by the bride's family. Neither Viv not her son seemed to be much involved in any of the planning; in fact Viv had refused an invitation to look with her future daughter-in-law at a wedding dress, because she finds the whole excitement about things like that slightly "naff". In fact, the whole wedding and everything that she had heard about it felt slightly naff to her: the money involved, the "celebrity wedding" style ("there will be doves, no doubt!"), and, though it was never directly said, her daughter-in-law seemed to be included in this description. She was described as nice and competent, but words like talented, intelligent and sophisticated were reserved for her son. Viv would have wished for something else for him, and again, whilst this comment referred to the wedding, I could not help but feel this may extend to her future daughter-in-law too, who seemed to be rather damned with faint praise.

Only further into the conversation did I hear about Viv's own first marriage to her son's father: he had been seen by his parents as the intelligent, cultured and sophisticated party and at that time it was Viv whose competence and niceness was clearly seen by them as inferior and the marriage as a bit of a compromise. Further back in her childhood there was also an older brother who was their parents' favourite. A working-class family, they adored and indulged this son who was the first in his family to go to university. Viv also went to university, but this seemed to have been noticed less. Her role in her family of origin was to be the one who did not cause any trouble or excitement.

Any hurt about this was only hinted at and, if talked about at all, then again it was in a tone of slightly bemused detachment. It was clear that both this detachment and a fierce determination to become the truly intelligent, successful, talented and sophisticated one in this "competition" had been Viv's coping devices. "Golden boy" brother did not do so well after all, and Viv's ex-husband's business ventures failed one after the other in spite of his "brilliance". It was Viv who had created this life and this room and she was at ease with it: it was hers.

The wedding and her attitude to it could then be seen as another way of re-visiting a past conflict, only this time with reversed roles. This time it was Viv who, through her son, was on the side of "golden boys", in a position to look safely down, rather than be looked down upon. It allowed her in a subtle way to rewrite history. I do not think that Viv was aware that this may be what she was doing, but she nevertheless drew satisfaction and relief from being on the other side, reversing a painful and traumatic pattern of her past.

I was repeatedly aware in these interviews that I was treading a fine line between just gathering information and neutral listening on the one hand and on the other hand pointing out some of the parallels I was observing. This is what I would do as a psychotherapist in my interactions with clients, but of course I was not these women's therapist. Occasionally I tentatively offered some of my observations. Perhaps not surprisingly the effect was not that dissimilar to what can happen in therapy: almost without exception, the woman in question was intrigued by the parallel, often something seemed to click and even lead to some relief. Making sense of your own reactions and behaviour is almost always helpful. Indeed this kind of awareness may be the best chance we have as mothers to disentangle some of the complications in our relationships with our adult children and their partners.

What to do and how to be

- Check in with yourself and ask probing questions. Is this happening to me for the first time? This seems to me one crucial question to ask when we find ourselves stuck in a loop of fear, resentment and rather intense feelings. Is it possible that you feel that strongly about something because you have been here before? Is it the past that hurts rather than just the present? Knowing this does not mean your feelings will disappear but you may give yourself the chance to distinguish between what belongs in the here and now and what does not. It will calm things down and give you a chance to step back.

- Don't predict outcomes. You are not caught in inevitable repeat loops, particularly not once you understand what is happening and what feeds your feelings.

- Don't over-dramatise: families, even the best functioning ones, are not conflict free. You can disagree on things, you can hate each other from time to time; that is all quite normal. Do not believe what you are told of families who are living in the glow of constant harmony. That is for Instagram!

Chapter 5

Me, myself, I

Whether their children settle with partners, whether their children have children of their own, whether the relationship between adult child and mother has moved successfully into a more mature way of relating to each other, one task remains the same for all mothers at this stage of the family life cycle: they need to and often want to find something that gives them an identity beyond being a mother. If they have stepped back, as they need to do, some space will have opened up again that will need to be filled. The "empty nest" image implies a confusion about purpose, an absence of old routines, pleasures and responsibilities. This leaves mothers with a space that can feel both frightening and exciting. If moving towards the margins of your child's life is the task, if it is also about getting used to and tolerating being an observer rather than a participant in their lives, then the question is: who am I when I am this observer at the margins? Where is the centre of my own life?

> Maggie puts it like this: *"If I am not the centre of their world any more, they cannot be the centre of mine."*
>
> Susan: *"I am not sitting on the sofa waiting for a phone call."*
>
> Jacqueline: *"When all that space opened up, I thought 'I can do something for me now'."*
>
> Sarah: *"I needed to reassess my own life. I thought I can do now what I want to do, but I did not know what I wanted to do."*

This is the crucial question: what *do* these mothers want to do when all this space opens up? Who do they want to be? There are various stages of life when this question may have arisen already and with increasing urgency. For some mothers it has occurred and been answered when the children went to school and these mothers may have caught up with interrupted careers or intensified their engagement with them. For some it happened at later stages, maybe with their child's adolescence, certainly with their child leaving home. Interestingly, for women this tends to coincide with a physical event that powerfully influences the way they are likely to feel about this stage of their life and their family's development, namely the menopause. The menopause has strong physical, social and emotional dimensions. Calling it "the change" encompasses all of these. At its centre there is indeed the task of coming to terms with an enormous change. It does not just signal the end of a woman's childbearing years, but for women who have born and brought up children it tends to coincide with the enormous change of their role in relationship to those children, which this book is concerned with. The social and emotional change forces women to face questions of ageing, of redefinition of core relationships and, especially in Western society, with potentially waning power and status. Hormonal changes may lend an emotional fragility to this stage, but the questions asked are often rather concerned with a midlife assessment. What have I done with my life so far? What am I going to do with the rest of it? We could add to this for women who are mothers: who am I now that my children are growing up and I am not needed in the way I was before? For some women this leads to a wish to link up with their pre-mother self.

Angie: *"I'm getting back to the former me."*

This view often goes hand in hand with a view of their lives as mothers where motherhood somehow interrupted a trajectory that may have taken them in a very different direction. It is still a fact that in general women's career prospects and earning power take more of a hit when they have children than men's when they become fathers. Women still tend to interrupt their work for longer periods; they may go part-time for years or change their work pattern to a rhythm that suits their responsibilities as parents. Once a pattern is established that makes fathers the main earners, decisions around location, distribution of labour in the house, etc. tend to follow the logic of the main earner, and women's priorities tend to be put on hold and take second position. I am not questioning that this is often the result of negotiations between both partners and it may be entirely what suits both of them, but undoubtedly that is not always the case. Certainly in midlife women in this position are facing a more daunting reality as far as their chances of "getting back to their former self" are concerned. Particularly those women who defined themselves predominantly around their role as mother face a crisis of identity when that role is not in such strong demand any more and there is no obvious or easy alternative. Some women seem to get stuck in a desperate attempt to hold back the tide and cling to their children and their lives in a battle that is often difficult and distressing for both parties. Some seem to stay in a state of limbo until grandmother-hood offers them the second chance they have been waiting for. What I have described before as confusion over generational boundaries and attempts to be the expert who knows better than the younger generation is often associated with this position.

Many others, however, interpret the possibility of getting back to their former self in a different way. They are looking for a change that allows them to fill the space that has opened up in their lives in a way that acknowledges that things have indeed changed, that they themselves have changed, and that the next phase in their lives offers them options that they wish to actively influence. This is hardly ever a quick process and hardly ever an easy and comfortable one.

Work, retraining, moving in a completely different career direction or reinvesting in the existing career were the most often mentioned paths in my interviews. The reality of the labour market does not make this easy, and yet a lot of the mothers I spoke to mentioned work as a way forward for themselves.

> "*My daughter's wedding was a marker for change. I needed to do something,*" says Debbie who subsequently started training as a counsellor.

> Carole: "*I just buried myself in work. At work I could deal with a crisis, provide a solution, the absolute opposite to my private life.*"

> Sandra: "*In the end I retrained and that was a saviour. Work became my rock.*"

> Maggie: "*I gave my mind something to do that had nothing to do with my daughter.*"

> Angie: "*I do have a life of my own, my children aren't my life. I get out, I do my own things.*"

Doing one's on thing does not necessarily mean working: top of the list in my interviews was connecting or reconnecting with friends.

> Diane: "*Friends, it is so important to normalise these things, bonding with other women who go through similar things.*"

> Elenor: "*Friends become the main support structure rather than family, they come back into view when family is not the centre of our life any more and we are not part of theirs.*"

Energy that has been taken up with looking after the family is available for friends again, so is time, particularly for those mothers who have retired or who have not engaged with work again. Existing friendships were revived and new ones formed, often associated with new activities and hobbies. There was a distinctive shift in evaluating those friendships. After years of putting the family first and friends fitting in if and when possible, now is the time for friendships taking centre stage again, in that way catching up with a way of life that had been dominant pre children. There may also be a renewed investment in contact with extended family of the same generation. Friendships were associated with support, but also with having fun, with a lighter, more playful, quality shining through. What many mothers mentioned was the mutual support structure in friendships, different from the more one-directional quality of the mother/child relationship, which is repeatedly commented on by mothers.

> Susan: *"My children, they expect me to be there for them, they are not selfish, and they just do. My friends, we are there for each other."*

This mutual support provides an important counterweight to the experience of being a mother, establishing a balance that had been tilted for many mothers for quite a while.

There is also a changing experience of marriage and relationships. Marriages and relationships may not survive this stage and there is a substantial number of separations amongst empty nesters. Some women may bring a new partner into the family which can set off a multitude of problems with adult children. Relationships and marriages that survive this stage can take on a different life, with many women reporting rediscovering each other again after years of being part of the working unit "family". Travelling together and holidays are mentioned a lot, whether that involves buying a camper van, going to a music festival, booking a cruise or a bus holiday. Some who can afford it have bought second homes abroad to overwinter; others book more exotic holidays than they may have been able to take with the family. Socialising together as a couple figures highly, going to the pub, to the cinema, meeting with friends, often just enjoying each other's company without the extra stresses that living with children and particularly teenagers can bring. There is often a new appreciation of the passing of time and wanting to make the most of the remaining years together.

> Emily: *"At the end of the day the years of bringing up the children are actually not that long. You are a couple before they come along, then you think this will go on forever, living together as a family, but then they are gone and you are a couple again and you have to find out whether that is still enough. That can be a bit scary."*

> Lilian: *"Who knows how much time we have left? I don't want to waste that, by worrying, by focusing on the wrong stuff, by having the wrong priorities, by just thinking, we can do that later. We may not!"*

Often this time will bring the extra challenge of retirement, another change that involves a crisis of identity. Finding new projects, separate and together, and having strong friendship networks seem to be the best guarantors of women and couples alike weathering this time of upheaval. It is important to note that these changes are not linked to the grown-up children and they are allowing an identity that is separate from the roles people have in their families. In fact this separate identity is enjoyed by some of the mothers with a nearly "naughty pleasure" quality to it.

> Wendy, whose son got married abroad, tells me triumphantly how she and her husband combined the wedding with a holiday: *"They had their wedding, but we had our own road trip, yay!"*

Maybe not surprisingly, forging out a new path for oneself can lead to clashes with the ongoing needs of the family. The on/off nature of the connection with grown-up children is something that many mothers have commented on before. Grown-up children may lead their lives for long stretches of time with only minimal contact, and the mothers may wonder at times quite where they figure. Then things can change very rapidly: their child presents with a crisis, be it practical, financial or emotional; an event like a new partner, a pregnancy, a job loss or career move, and all of a sudden mothers find themselves in the spotlight of their adult child's attention and possibly their need. Most mothers will want to respond to this, and often they report dropping everything else and going into full scale "mummy bear" mode, as one of the mothers called it.

Erica: *"It is so nice to feel they still need you from time to time."*

Sandra: *"The best thing is when you feel they still want you in their life."*

Being needed again feels good, particularly as a lot of the mothers seem to feel a considerable amount of anxiety around whether their help and support is welcome and whether they are getting it right. They tell of time spent agonising whether they gave too little, or too much, or whether it was the right thing.

Amrita: *"You have to be careful not to over-give."*

This can concern gifts, but also just conversations or reactions to events in their child's life, and many mothers admit to being plagued by ruminating self-doubt about getting it right. This is not helped by the fact that knowing each other well leads to picking up any signs of irritation or criticism, a fact particularly commented on by mothers of daughters.

Deborah was told by her daughter about her engagement. *"I asked, can I tell people in the family or would you like to tell them? She said, no, you are welcome to tell them, but I don't want everybody bombarding me with questions. As if that was somehow down to me. And I felt somehow I had got it wrong again."*

It is therefore with some enthusiasm that mothers seem to respond when the child sends a clear signal: I would like your support, it is welcome.

> Angie: *"He is really appreciative of my help at the moment. That won't last..."* (*she laughs*).

For some mothers, however, the child's asking for support can cause dilemmas, particularly those mothers who had been successful in forging new identities and projects for themselves. Working out how to respond to these distress calls is not always easy. Many mothers reported that they found their children's attitude at time amusing, at times exhausting.

> Helen: *"They want you off their back, you are just too much for them, your attention is like pressure. They want you to 'get a life'. Then they want you for something and they are quite taken aback that you may actually have a life now, and that you may not wish to put it on hold just like that."*

> Grace: *"I think they expected our lives to stand still. Our assignment was to stagnate and live in the past, and when we didn't, well, not always easy, it seems!"*

Short Story
Demand-feeding

It had been the usual flight from Gatwick, early in the morning, having left the house just before dawn. Holidays often seemed to start like this, tension building up during the last days before departure, trying to remember what to pack, what to organise before leaving the house, ticking items on an ancient list on the back of an envelope as she went.

The older Barbara got, the more there was a background anxiety creeping into her preparations that she could not quite explain. If anything, things were so much easier as far as travelling was concerned, now that it was just herself and Richard. Once in Gatwick, the anxiety had given way to the familiar state of airport anaesthetics, zoning out mentally. Neither of them talked much, comfortable in the knowledge that there would be plenty of time to talk once they were in their hotel. She had eaten her stale croissant and played with her phone, looking at yesterday's text exchanges with her daughter. There had been a flurry of them, panicked and urgent, but for once she had managed to say she would deal with this later.

It was curious how often there was something urgent going on in her children's lives just before she was about to go away, a conference, a holiday or a social engagement. It was as if they sensed her moving away, like they had sensed her tiptoeing out of the room when they were babies and she thought they may have settled and give her a break.

Once at the hotel, Barbara showered and put on a dress that always cheered her up, and walked to the tapas bar where Richard would be joining her later. Sipping her wine she watched people, locals and tourists walking past. A couple caught her eye who were dressed in colourful hippy clothes, their hair long and un-styled, caught in some time warp of their youth. They turned and called for a teenage girl to catch up with them. The girl was also dressed in an exuberant hippy style and Barbara realised how certain she had been that any daughter of this couple would be faintly embarrassed by her parents. To the contrary, this girl seemed to be rather following her parents' lead and the three of them looked like a very harmonious unit. Barbara sighed: how had they managed? Before her thoughts had

had a chance to go into a troubling repeat loop, Richard appeared. He ordered a beer and, while they were waiting for it to arrive, they looked at each other for the first time since they had started their journey and both started laughing.

The last couple of months had been full on: Richard had finally decided to go for early retirement, but the last months of trying to clear his desk and hand things over neatly to his successor had been more stressful than they had imagined. Of course it was a big decision, not just financially: retirement is not an easy, straightforward stage of life and Richard had been simultaneously both anxious and looking forward to it. She herself had taken the plunge more gently last year, reducing her hours and shifting the focus of her work. She had had several phases in her life when work had not been the dominating factor. Maternity leave, a period of redundancy and then building up freelance work had seen to that. Retirement therefore did not have quite the same associations of getting older as it clearly had for Richard who seemed at times to be rather at a loss.

It was probably a bit much to expect the children to understand any of that. They were at such different stages of their lives. What they seemed to sense though was that their parents' availability might be up for grabs. Last night's texts were very much in that vein. Sophie's childminder was pregnant, she was having a difficult time with it and would have to stop working for quite a while, starting soon. Could Barbara and Richard possibly help out, and how often and for how long? Sophie was frantic as to how to find cover for the twins, and she really did not want to consider nursery childcare. It would help ever so much, if they could tell her, the sooner the better.

Barbara adored her grandsons, loved to visit. Looking after them was a pleasure, not a burden. She would love to help her daughter, but to commit on a regular basis? There were so many grandmothers who seemed to do this nowadays, but was that really what she wanted for herself right now? Was she indeed entitled to think about what she wanted for herself?

Their food arrived, spicy sausage, small fried peppers and anchovies, bread with roasted tomatoes and plenty of garlic and olive oil. Food to wake you up and make you smile and feel that maybe all is well after all, its foreignness a protective layer against any temptation to let her thoughts get caught up in the net of her daughter's childcare arrangements and her son's trouble in deciding about his job. Which had been the subject of a long conversation the evening before, not contributing to her ability to look forward to the holiday.

When she woke up the next day Barbara felt a sense of relaxation she had not felt for a while. They had done it, the pressure of the last weeks behind them, a beautiful late summer's day ahead of them with nothing to do but decide whether to go for a swim and where to eat. At last there would be time to concentrate on the two of them, as a couple rather than as parents, which seemed to have been rather difficult recently. Focus on the present, your own life; the children are adults and can sort their own lives out: easier said than done somehow. They bought some fresh bread, cheese and some peaches and set off for a hike down to the coast. Apart from a couple of serious walkers in bright high-tech outfits they did not meet many people. The sun had that late summer quality that gives the colours both clarity and softness and through the pine forests they could at every corner see the sea sparkling in the distance. With every step her thoughts seemed to become quieter and she found herself just walking and watching and listening. By the time they reached the beach they were hot and sweaty and a couple of minutes later she was into her swimsuit and wading into the warm Mediterranean Sea. There was something about this kind of walking and this kind of swimming that made you live in your body and enjoy it. Questions of looking "right" or not were not of any relevance. Good sex of course did the same to you. It was the opposite of seeing your body as an adversary that had to be fought and trained and controlled, as Sophie seemed now to do all of the time... She noticed how her thoughts were yet again drawn back to her daughter, and the beach and the sea paled into the background.

Sophie's need for her mother was a complicated beast. There were times when she seemed to hardly remember her mother's existence and Barbara felt both released and discarded, reminding herself that it was good for both of them to learn to be independent, and that in order to be truly capable of relating to each other as adults they had to learn distance from each other first. Yet just when that became easier and Barbara was focusing on her own non-mother life again, with a degree of ambivalence but not without pleasure, Sophie would knock on her door again. There was never a hint of hesitation or indeed a question over whether her mother would drop everything to respond – which was both lovely and irritating. Or maybe what was really puzzling was that she, Barbara, would indeed drop everything to respond without much hesitation or assessment of the importance of whatever the current issue that her daughter laid on her table.

She remembered being pregnant with Sophie, still with enough time to do yoga most evenings. Subsequent pregnancies had not held that luxury. She had sat there cross-legged in her bedroom, aware of the nest of house martins in the eaves of the roof. The fledglings were waiting for their mother and the moment she arrived their little beaks were gaping and their demanding noise left no doubt that they wanted food and they wanted it now. She had found that very funny and moving. Later, when the baby was there, she often thought of the little birds when she heard the baby starting to stir, soon to rev up to a full demanding roar. Staggering out of bed, sometimes feeling nearly sick with tiredness, she had nevertheless loved the tenderness of those night feeds when there was nobody else there in the still dark hours in the depth of the night but the two of them, feeding. Demand-feeding had been the phrase, responding to your baby's demand, rather than imposing your own schedule, your own need for routine and breaks. Child-centred, that had been another phrase, and she never had any doubt that was what a small child deserved and your own needs just had to step into the background for a while. She had never regretted that, but she was sometimes shocked at the ferocity of her adult children's wide open beaks!

She was not on her own in this; most of her friends had tales to tell. Some would not hesitate to drop everything, including their friends, if their adult child needed or wanted a feed. Some tried to negotiate a balance, but all found it complicated. The babies had needed their feeds and deserved their mothers' ability and willingness to respond quickly, to read their babies' needs correctly. This demand-feeding of adult children was a different story. Wherever she looked there seemed to be this push/pull of the mother–child interaction, the constant hot and cold of "don't come too close, don't interfere, this is my life" and then "I'm struggling, can you help?" or "look, I have done this, aren't *you proud?" You could sense the mothers' anxiety in the background: we must not miss the opportunity when it arises. It may not come again so soon, and not to respond to the demand may lead to further distance, to mothers becoming more and more redundant. Admitting that essentially the child may not need you anymore to solve their problems and therefore pulling back is by no means easy: in fact it can feel like a different kind of retirement. Too early? Always too early?*

Barbara tried to wave away the uninvited thought-clouds that had formed. She tried to get back to the beach, to Richard, to this moment, out of the loop of her worries about her daughter's childcare arrangements, her son's job decisions, running in the background of her mind like a powerful film in constant repeat, imposing itself between her and Richard, between her and the beach, between her and her own life.

Was it time to finally move the baby into the nursery and close the bedroom door?

As this short story indicates, boundaries which may have had to be redefined before, often painfully so, are now again in a constant state of negotiation and renegotiation. What to do with the space left behind by the adult child and where to draw the line is never straightforward, even in its literal meaning: the same child that may be adamant that she is now officially leaving and setting up home somewhere else may still be extremely reluctant to take her belongings with her. My interviews were full of remarks about adult children's possessions still being stored in the parental home and parents being made to feel quite unreasonable if they felt it was time the son or daughter took their boxes away. Clearing out a "child's" bedroom and using it for other purposes – a guestroom, a study, a work room of some sort – or downsizing to a different house or flat was felt to be a difficult step to take by the mothers who saw it as a final acknowledgement of a change that had taken place. It was also often a strong statement about the space being now the mother's, and her filling it with her own non-mother identity. It was perhaps more surprisingly greeted with hardly concealed disapproval and dismay by many of the adult sons and daughters, often those who had been quite vociferous in their wish for independence and separation. Mothers filling the gap in other ways, as described above, by reviving friendships, reinvesting in work and projects or increased leisure activities can all provoke this at best ambivalent and at worst shocked or hostile response.

Adult children often seemed to struggle with their mothers' new active life away from them. Specifically, they often seemed to be supportive in general, but more bothered in detail: a mother's travel plans or work plans seemed to be welcomed, but more of a bother when it became clear that this might clash with help for childcare. Mother's having a good friendship group was good news in that they were not looking to the adult child for too much attention, but could also draw hardly hidden criticism, often from daughters:

"You and your friends..."

"You talk about everything with your friends, don't you?"

"Meeting for lunch again?"

All of the above were reported by the mothers to be said in rather tart tones.

The fact that the older generation often has more time available and in many cases more disposable income compared to the adult child who may be stuck in the time and financial demands of having a young family seems to lead to envy, mothers and daughters being more prone to this. One of my interviewees told of how her daughter had declared herself repeatedly supportive of her mother's newly developed "career" as an online cookery writer, but somehow consistently failed to find the time to look at any of her mother's published recipes. Another mother had come to the conclusion that she had to be very careful about sending her daughter any WhatsApp photos from a holiday as this had drawn "Well, it's fine for some" comments. A third remembered her daughter being rather critical of her and her friends laughing rather too loudly in the kitchen for her daughter's liking. Another one added that her own weight loss as a result of a renewed emphasis on exercise and fitness had got a rather hostile response from her daughter who struggled as a young mother with her weight.

What all of the mothers found hard was the contrast between what they would have expected of themselves in terms of showing interest and providing support towards their child and the rather surly response they got from their child toward their own interests. Being told of laughing too loudly in the kitchen after years of putting up with teenage sleepovers, not having one's recipes read after years of reading every single one of the child's poems and admiring her drawings, limiting one's photo output on WhatsApp after years of looking at photos sent by the child from their travels: it is the discrepancy that was commented on, the continuation of the one-way traffic of communication and attention.

So, while being needed was on the whole experienced as positive, there was also a general acknowledgement that negotiating boundaries was an ongoing task during the time of their children's adult lives. The question of when to respond and when not to, of how to fill the space vacated by the child, and how to establish a relationship in which both sides were comfortable in their separate lives and able to show mutual interest and support, stayed as a work in progress for most mothers I spoke with.

It seemed as if both mothers and children subconsciously acknowledged that the change into adult independence is somehow supposed to be driven by the young adult who takes increasing control of events. If it was the mothers who "took back control" and filled the space left behind, then that seemed to require some more complicated readjustment on both sides.

What to do and how to be

- Change always implies an element of loss. Adjusting to our children growing up means we have to deal with a momentous and ongoing change. It does not help to pretend this does not involve loss and mourning for times gone by. On the contrary it is only normal and certainly not a sign of failure. Denial never works in the long run, so give yourself permission to at times feel sad, often confused and at a loss. The more you just fight it by pretending it is not happening, the more it is likely to come back to bite you when you least expect it.

- Change opens up new spaces which you have a chance to fill. You may not know straight away what it is you may want to do or be, but keep looking. This could be your time, as a person, as a couple, as a friend.

- Be prepared for unpredictable reactions: your adult children may have quite an ambivalent attitude to the changing attitude you may adopt to your own life. They may be generally supportive, but struggle with the detail of your potentially waning availability.

- If you can, allow for flexibility: negotiating how much you want to be available to your children's needs is a surprisingly difficult process and takes time. Be clear with yourself and them how much you can and are prepared to offer. It is possible to say no.

- Your adult child may be at a stage of their life where demands of career and parenthood or just "life" are quite difficult. You may have more freedom right now, more choices: prepare for a certain amount of unacknowledged envy.

Chapter 6

Acceptance

For a mother of an adult child to be comfortable in her own identity and one that is not completely tied up with being a mother and to exist at a satisfactory, safe yet flexible distance from her adult child requires dealing with one of the biggest challenges of motherhood: mothers will have to accept the reality of their now adult child, to see them as the adult they now are, not the adult the mothers may have expected or wished them to become. Throughout the interviews I could hear a sometimes faint, sometimes louder, refrain: "Where has the child gone that I knew?" Parenting creates an intimate and passionate relationship, albeit one in which one partner constantly and dramatically changes, from baby to toddler, from toddler to pre-school child, from child to adolescent, and from adolescent to grown-up.

I carried out a personal project recently that involved ordering and digitalising family photos. It was an awesome process to go through the years and be reminded of my children changing. How could these be the same people, this soft little boy and now this tall young man who needs to bend down now to give me one of his amazing hugs, this chubby little girl and now the lithe young woman who competently runs her life and has two children of her own? Of course there are characteristics running through even just the images, and certainly my memories join them up as the same people, yet the change is formidable and our relationship with our children has to shift, our love for them has to change, our relationship with them cannot stay the same. "I know him", mothers say, and they do and yet there is so much they do not know about the grown-up who was once their baby. Maybe one of the biggest challenges is how to deal with the need to gradually give up our idealisation of our children, our hopes and ambitions for them, and accept that this is exactly what they were: *our* hopes and ambitions, not necessarily *theirs*. "I am so proud of him/her" mothers may say, but what if they are not? What if the beautiful baby has grown into an awkward teenager and now a rather unappealing grown-up? What if the grown-up child does not at all fit what his/her mother values as attractive qualities in a person? What if there is a clash over political opinions, about religion, about values, attitudes, lifestyle or just taste? What if the child settles with a partner who really does not fit in with the family culture, if they bring up their children in a way the grandmother cannot approve of? What if the child becomes more and more different from what the mother expected when her child was still all promise? If a long-standing friend changes in a way that stretches what both parties have in common, the friendship often fades away. Children and parents are linked in a way that makes that less of an option. "You cannot really divorce your children", as one of my interviewees put it. Even the mothers who are perfectly happy with their child's choices still often marvel at "the stranger" their child is to them at times. How to continue to love when the people involved are changing so much?

Early transitional years are still very much characterised by mothers feeling that they need to influence their children's choices, or at least be active in helping them make good ones and not sabotage their future chances. This can be observed particularly in the way parents view educational decisions of their teenagers or their friendship and partner choices. Gradually, however, they necessarily play a smaller part in their children's lives and become observers. The question seems to be whether parents and, for the purpose of this book, mothers in particular, can truly accept that their adult child may choose a life that may be right for the child, even if it would not be for the mother. Some mothers were capable

of distinguishing between the two, but often the "But I know him/
her so well" blurred the boundary. Did they really still know their
child that well? Could they truly accept that this was an adult with
a separate identity?

Often mothers in my interviews described their children as if the
adult child was only prevented by circumstances from becoming
the person he/she was supposed to be in the mother's eyes and it
was only going to be a matter of time before the transformation was
going to be achieved. Friends were blamed, partners very often.
Mothers were hoping for career changes, more suitable partners,
maybe that just getting older would reset everything.

> Maria: "*I just wish he got out of that friendship group. None of them
> have any ambition, they are all just drifting.*"

> Tina: "*Ever since he has been with her, he has been just not interested
> any more in his old life. He used to be so curious and enterprising...
> not any more.*"

> Erica: "*I never thought she would settle for that kind of life. She is so
> bright, but she does not seem to want to use her brain. It's all children
> and church. I cannot bear it.*"

> Olga: "*She is still young, things can change, maybe she will grow out
> of this romantic idea of what her life should be like.*"

Further down the line mothers struggle to come to terms with the
fact that this after all may be the kind of person their child is going
to be, this may be the life that they may want to lead or are going
to lead.

It seems to me that for a successful relationship between adult
child and mother one task is crucial. In order to develop a successful
relationship between any two adults several things have to happen:
both parties have to accept the reality of the other as a separate
person, a person one knows well and yet a stranger at the same

time. Disappointment as a feeling is commonly defined as sadness caused by the non-fulfilment of one's own hopes and expectations. Maybe the kind of disappointment that is involved in letting go of maternal expectations may be a difficult but necessary step towards acceptance of our children as separate people. Only from that point onwards can the one-way traffic of concern and care be interrupted. Both parties will have to allow their preconceptions about each other to change and to stop holding each other prisoner in a web of nostalgic love mixed up with resentment.

Short Story
Without memory or desire

The phrase had stuck in her mind: "without memory or desire". Julia's therapist had used it, even though Julia could not remember the context. She had been attending regular psychotherapy sessions for a while when she really felt she was going under. Teenagers at home, her mother needing more and more help and all that against the background of the menopause. She had felt so alone with it: her husband had somehow decided that her battles with Poppy were just a "mother/daughter thing" and her brother seemed to think that responding to their mother's increasing frailty and demandingness was also somehow a "mother/daughter thing". So in the end she decided to pay for help and found this therapist who clearly agreed that this was indeed a mother/daughter thing. This time though Julia had not been expected to do anything in particular. That is where this "without memory or desire" must have figured. Week after week on drizzly autumn and winter evenings she would drive to this woman's office, climb up the stairs, sit down and the therapist would listen to her and help her think about what was going on, seemingly without any desire for Julia to arrive anywhere in particular. Julia could still remember the room, the smell of it, and it made her feel a bit calmer even now.

That was some time ago now, but it was the same drizzly rain falling now while she was driving back home from seeing Poppy.

She remembered deciding on the name Poppy: her other two children had solid, deliberately bland names. She had been so keen not to pass on any expectations that a name can hold, so keen to let her children be what they wanted to be and not let her own wishes and hopes interfere. As it happened, George and Ella had on the whole turned out to be the way she may have wished for. Julia and her husband were both teachers and George and Ella had fitted without any pressure into a family culture that valued books and conversations and work. Of course they had had their moments of teenage rebellion, but on the whole their life choices had made for an easy fit. Ella had trained as a nurse, George worked in local government; they had turned into nice, responsible, emotionally competent adults. They had chosen partners who merged into the family with pleasing ease, and coming back from visits to either of her older children's homes tended to leave Julia with a warm afterglow, quite different from the tension she felt when driving back from Poppy's.

Poppy... it was a different name, it had felt a bit playful and they had not thought about it for ages, as they had with the other two, just gone for it when they first saw her. They had not really planned for another baby, but when she arrived, with her little face like a crumpled flower opening up after the rain, she had said "hello Poppy" and it had stuck. Poppy had stayed different from the other two somehow, different from herself and her husband also. She *was a dreamy little thing, not really able or willing to fit into any routine, not able or willing to focus easily on anything but her own dreamy creations. "I must not rush her," Julia had often thought and she had found it painful to see how increasingly the world expected Poppy to fit in with routines and targets. Schools were not made for the Poppys of this world. Poppy got frustrated, got angry, she turned into a child that was seen as a problem and Julia was not sure how to help. Part of her was frustrated too, willing Poppy on to just comply a bit more, to make a bit more of an effort.* It would not hurt to give them something, to do some of the work and keep dreaming and playing and creativity for another corner of your life, *she thought and said to Poppy,* just like the rest of us have to do. *George and Ella went from achievement to achievement, still keeping time for themselves and their friends and their hobbies, but Poppy did not seem to be able to draw the line. The whole idea of a distinction between work and hobby or leisure never became acceptable to her: she wanted to be "Poppy" full time. Part of Julia was perfectly happy with that at first. She had been proud of Poppy's otherness, her creative dreamy playful nature. She had very consciously resisted the urge to press Poppy into the straitjacket of expectations, or at least that is what she thought she had done. Maybe her expectations of her youngest daughter had been more subtle: she had most certainly looked at her and felt that she was somehow special, that she had a talent that somehow made her stand out, be a bit less of a plodder than the rest of her family. She had deep down expected that this specialness would eventually become visible to the world and that Julia's belief in her daughter would somehow be rewarded.*

As a girl, Poppy, who had been so sensitive to her surroundings, had created beautiful wild pictures which Julia put up everywhere in the house. The pictures had gradually become less beautiful and rather wilder, not of the kind you would want to look at all of the time. Poppy had become wilder. There were more and more clashes with teachers, falling outs with friends. Poppy's pictures and poems started telling a story of a mind that was not playful any more, but troubled, unhappy, overwhelmed by the chaos of her own thoughts and imagination. Could Julia have done something then to help her contain this chaos? She had seen two children through adolescence, but Poppy's teenage years felt different and Julia felt terrifyingly out of her depth. Poppy's chaos started to feel so scary that Julia observed herself responding in ways she did not understand, getting sucked into loud arguments with her daughter, filled with a rage and fear that seemed quite out of control. Then she felt the urge to push back, the urge to provide as much structure and order and calmness for her daughter as she could muster. Poppy did not want any of it. She blanked her mother as she had blanked out the world of school and formal expectations.

That is when the different friends started appearing; drugs, as far as she could tell, nothing heavy, but sure enough Poppy was self-medicating, as Julia's therapist had later called it. Julia's friends said "she will grow out of it, it is a phase, she is a teenager," trying to reassure her, but Julia knew that not all teenagers grow out of it. She saw it and she saw her daughter slipping away from her and from the safe life of her childhood and, as if in a nightmare, Julia could not move and she could not save her.

Then there had been a time when she started to hope her friends may be right: Poppy had applied to and had been accepted at Art School and Julia had held her breath, never quite ready to exhale.

The thing is, it is difficult to know whether you have reached the point when you can afford to exhale. Poppy had eventually dropped out of Art School, she had travelled a bit, slightly perfunctorily, and then settled down to a life of casual jobs and a life that was rather a mystery to Julia.

The rain was getting heavier and Julia decided to stop for a coffee. She ran from the car into the service station, full of other drivers with empty eyes, children squabbling, parents looking on with exhausted detachment. The coffee was bitter, the loos smelled of something peachy and chemical and the noise of the hand dryers drilled into your skull.

Wearily she thought of the shared house that Poppy now lived in. The state of Poppy's room... She thought of her therapist's room which had always made her feel calm and had somehow given her space to think in. Poppy's room was the opposite: if Poppy's mind was like this room, there was no space to feel calm enough to step back a bit and think. There was only chaos, overwhelming chaos.

Today though her daughter had looked well and relaxed. She had actually planned ahead and there was lunch, very nice vegan food. A couple of her friends had come by, looking very much like Poppy herself, with their tattoos, their dreadlocks, their shaggy and not very clean clothes. Julia had long stopped being shocked by the state of their teeth or by the weird names they all seemed to have. Some of them had jobs of sorts, but certainly nothing that could be described by any stretch of the imagination as a career. They had vague politics, green on the whole, with bits of various conspiracy theories thrown in for good measure. They were lovely and friendly, all of them one way or the other part of the eco scene, or music or art scene. Like Poppy, most of them would see smoking weed as being as normal as Julia's generation saw having a glass of wine in the evening. *Was it the weed that made them all rather mellow, but also seemingly lacking in any ambition or drive?*

This was definitely not an academic question. Whichever way you answered it, you made their attitude into something that was either a different but acceptable and respectable attitude to have, or you turned it into something that was the result of rather drug-befuddled brains, a side effect of weed and, as such, a problem. She could not decide on this one.

Neither could she decide therefore whether her own worry was completely justified, nor whether it was still her responsibility to think about how to help Poppy, to challenge her if necessary, maybe find her a therapist that Poppy could go to on damp and drizzly afternoons.

It was however possible that all this was only a problem to Julia and not to Poppy. It was possible that the problem was only with her own memory and desire, her memory of her golden dreamy child with her beauty and talent, her own desire for her special girl to become a success, to prove to the world that she was able to soar above the plodders, that she could do this when Julia herself had not. Poppy had chosen differently and who could say whether her life choice was a problem, a problem to whom anyway?

Julia left the service station and got back into the car. It would not take long before she was back in her own orderly world, leaving Poppy's world further and further behind.

You must be so proud of them, people said to Julia about Ella and George, as if the way they had turned out was her greatest maternal achievement.

Far away on the horizon dawned a realisation that maybe accepting disappointment was the real achievement; to let yourself be dis-appointed of your memory of who you thought your child was, and of your desire for what you wanted your child to be, but to see them, at last, for who they are, and desire nothing more than that.

What to do and how to be

- Remember that there is a difference between what you think would be right for your child and what they think would be right for themselves. It is so easy to project onto a child our own wishes, ambitions and fantasies, particularly when they are young. It is not their responsibility to live up to any of those! Accept that they have the right to be different from you.

- Try to see your child as a stranger from time to time, or a friend: would you be quite so forceful with your opinions, your assumptions, your thinking that you know them and that you know what is best for them?

- Remember also how you would expect to be treated by a friend or indeed a stranger. Try to be assertive about your own boundaries, do not pretend that your resources are limitless, communicate your own needs and insist on some turn-taking of interest and support. It may not be immediately successful, but it certainly will not change unless you try.

Chapter 7

Changing relationships

Being a mother of grown-up children involves having to accept, gradually but inevitably, that times are changing: it is the next generation's turn now and as the older generation we have to accept that our position in our families and in the generational field is shifting. Even in families where mothers still hold the position of powerful matriarch for quite some time, there comes the point when the older generation may grow frail and need support from their children.

During the recent pandemic something quite interesting seemed to be happening regarding the discourse about the relationship between the generations. Once it became clear that the virus was particularly dangerous to older people the language changed: seventy, or in some countries sixty-five, became the cut-off point for being described officially as "elderly" and thereby "vulnerable". The constant discussions around how to protect the elderly and vulnerable led to parallel shifts in perception in families of the older generation, often to the surprise of all participants. Grown-up children were asked to take on board their parents' vulnerability; parents were asked to accept both their own vulnerability and the corresponding concern or care offered by the younger generation. This proved to be not uncomplicated to say the least.

Short Story
In the vulnerable group

That she had not expected. Which was a ridiculous thing to say, as if anybody had been able to predict any of this: A global pandemic that had placed everybody at the centre of a science fiction film, waking up every morning wondering whether this was all really happening.

It was *happening* though. She stood at the window, for a long time looking out onto the by now familiar emptiness of her street: no car traffic, only the odd jogger running past. There were dog walkers following their daily routine as if nothing had changed, the odd couple striding out purposefully, regular joggers put out by parents running together with their children. They were all circling around each other, with a mixture of awkwardness, anxiety and irritation, glad to be out, probably equally glad to scuttle back into the safety of their homes. Mostly though the street was eerily empty and there was nobody to be seen at all.

What she hadn't expected was quite how her own life would change, the strange details of it all. She stared at her phone screen where the WhatsApp messages from her book group members were beginning to pop up. This would go on now, all through the day. Being barred from seeing each other, from seeing anybody outside of one's own household in fact, seemed to have unleashed wave after wave of connecting virtually. It had been such a boost in the early days to know that you were not on your own, that there were people out there who cared about you and who were part of your social and emotional network. Staying in touch through video calls and via messages and sharing *photos had made all the difference. Ping, another message: Nicola apparently had made more progress with her garden and her seedlings were doing well. More pings, and other group members were sending photos of their gardens. Wasn't it wonderful, all the birdsong, and wasn't the sky so much clearer now with less pollution, and hadn't the pace of life changed for the better? Erica had posted photos of her repainted garden furniture and the new table top, decorated with pieces of coloured glass which she had collected at the beach. The table sparkled in the sun, as did the glass of wine, lifted to say cheers, Erica with a beaming smile.*

She hesitated, thinking about how to respond, and wiped the worktops in the kitchen, again. What was mostly on her mind was the Zoom conversation she had had with her adult children over the weekend. The children now rang quite frequently and the weekend Zoom call, often combined with a family quiz, had become a regular feature of their week. She was touched by the fact that both her daughter and her son were clearly making an effort to stay in touch. She would not have taken that for granted after years of doing all the running, after years of wondering how long this one-way traffic of attention and effort between mother and adult child would continue. Something seemed to have shifted. As if the repeated talk of older people being more vulnerable to the virus had changed something in her children's perception of her. From being the invincible matriarch of unlimited resources, who could be called upon whenever there was a crisis, she seemed to have morphed within a month into an older person who was vulnerable. This was a new experience! Quite how she felt about it, she was not sure.

More WhatsApp messages: it clearly was exercise time in book group land. Monica had discovered online Zumba,

Moya had taken up running with the "from couch to 5k" app, all of them were jokingly contrasting their fitness regimes with the cocktails that would reward them in the evening, after some more creativity of some sort... None of them would come out of this without their cupboards sorted, their house spring cleaned, maybe a new language attempted... it was exhausting just listening to it. There was a breathless energy and speed to all this, a shrillness of enthusiasm, like a bunch of teenage girls getting ready for an outing, convincing each other how much fun they were having. Only of course there would not be an outing for quite some time and in reality all of them were near or over retirement age.

She herself kept reassuring her children that she was having fun or at least was coping well with lockdown and she had been quite surprised when it became clear that both of them had been talking about her, reassuring each other that she seemed to be doing really well. She had often been puzzled and disappointed in the past at how little interest and concern they seemed to be capable of as far as her life and her feelings were concerned. Careful what you wish for... yesterday she had told them how much she was looking forward to the hairdresser opening again in due course and having her roots done and a good cut. Her son had been quite forceful: what was she thinking of? Given her age, was a haircut really that important to take such a risk, with the virus still being out there and, again, at her age? She could, with some effort, with some considerable effort, remind herself that this comment came from a place of concern and a wanting to see her safe. And yet... since when had anybody been in a position to tell her whether to go to the hairdresser or not! This almost felt like a different kind of adolescence.

The doorbell rang and it was the food delivery. Julia put on her mask before opening the door. One had to think about every little move, every little interaction now. Safe, unsafe? Trustworthy, untrustworthy? Not everybody came to the same conclusion of course and her exchanges with others were accompanied by this slight sense of unease: was she being judged for being too anxious or too risk-taking? She certainly found herself judging others, if only silently. Julia in her book group posted happy pictures of herself and her granddaughter in her garden, where the granddaughter was definitely not meant to be. We were of course taking precautions, Julia posted cheerfully, as if this was some kind of reassurance about practising safe sex. Talking of sex, Julia and her husband clearly had plenty of it at the moment, as hinted at in Julia's WhatsApp contributions. It was as if there was a competition going on, the winner having the best and most creative, productive and enjoyable pandemic,.whilst most of them were at the same time being categorised as vulnerable, because of their asthma, their weight, their levels of fitness, their age...

Actually it was difficult to know what age anybody was at the moment. Her book group friends seemed to reside in some adolescent mania; she was herself all of a sudden and persistently identified as elderly, but at the same time was being treated like an unreasonable adolescent by her son who had come over all paternal. It could certainly feel confusing.

Her own mother had moved into a care home in her late eighties and it had been a relief when that happened. Her mother had not managed her affairs very well any more and she remembered with a pang of guilt how she had been exasperated by her mother signing up for an expensive and unnecessary subscription. Her impatience had shown and her mother had been upset. "You make me feel like I am stupid and incompetent." Thinking about it now, her frustration had certainly been rooted in trying to keep her mother safe, and yet, of course she probably had been patronising at times. At some stage you had to take on a more parental function with your own elderly parents. At some stage she would be on the receiving end of this, but this surely would be a gradual process, or so she had assumed. But now here it was, a change materialising within weeks: her son seemed to have been one minute hardly capable of keeping her in mind as another adult with needs and feelings, allowing him to stay in a semi adolescent country of switching mum on and off in a perfectly affectionate, but nevertheless completely self-centred way; the next minute he had moved into a position where he showed concern for her welfare, but in a manner that had a caring bossiness and a distinctively patronising tone. She had not expected it like that and not that suddenly.

Her daughter had been less vociferous in her criticism. With three young children and a demanding job, working from home and home schooling, with a husband who seemed quite unperturbed by any doubts as to whose job was more important (his, of course), she hardly had the energy to engage in debates about the importance of hairdressing appointments versus the risk of the virus. People are dying here, her son had pointed out, as if that may have somehow escaped her notice. Maybe being married to a fairly pompous man made her daughter a bit reluctant to join her brother. Trying to get out of the turn the Zoom conversation with her son was taking, she had joked "yes, Daddy," a joke that seemed to fall flat, though to her relief there had been a short laugh from her daughter. A father talking down to her like a slightly foolish young girl, a pompous man patronising her: was this the shape of things to come when being vulnerable and elderly robbed you of the option of telling them to mind their own business?

It was confusing to say the least, this sudden move into a different age category which changed how she saw herself and clearly how her children saw her. In the meantime her book group friends were still dancing on the Titanic, outdoing each other in their positive attitude. There were more WhatsApp messages, but she decided not to open them. She knew what they would say: loss, what loss? Vulnerability, whose vulnerability? Illness will not come, old age will not come, death will not come, not to us, because our energy and positive spirit is our vaccine. Feeling fear and sadness somehow seemed to have become a failure of character, an indication of low moral immunity.

In the background on the radio there was a discussion after the latest government briefing: politicians following "the science", the language of shielding, protecting the vulnerable... She was about to switch it off when an angry man in his late twenties started arguing that the baby boomer generation had not just done irreparable damage to the planet, benefitted from the huge house price rises, and left the younger generation with few chances and an enormous task to clear up the mess, but now the entire economy was in freefall as result of the lockdown measures. These measures are only necessary to protect the old people; again we are paying for them, he said. There was so much anger between the generations, and all the talk of shielding and protection of the old people had a dimension to it that did not feel entirely benign. There were scores to be settled here, between her and her son, as there had been between herself and her mother. The tables get turned, the boot is on the other foot now, what

> went around comes around. Care? Power? Love? These
> three remain...which one was it to be? How would they all
> come out of lockdown when inside it so much had been
> changed?
>
> She decided to pick up her phone, to ignore the WhatsApp
> book group, and started to write a friendly message to her
> son, appreciating his concern. After that she looked for the
> number of her hairdresser.

What this short story hints at is how complicated this sudden shift in perspective is for both parties. With very few exceptions, mothers in my interviews had described the relationships between themselves and their children up to now as a bit of a one-way traffic: concern, care and support were expected to be given by the mother to the child, even when the child was by now grown up.

Olga: *"He [son] rings when he wants something."*

Erica: *"The line of provision goes only one way with him, my daughter became an adult a bit earlier."*

Maggie: *"It is a bit of a one-way traffic of support. I'm there to help, but we don't meet socially."*

Deborah: *"My daughter-in-law is a bit more aware, she is a social worker."*

Carrie: *"I have health problems, but the children don't get it. I think they don't want to get it. It has been like that forever. They have never worried about asking for help."*

Christine: *"I'm too strong and she finds that difficult, and then I'm not strong enough and that is difficult too. She does not seem to be able to give me anything."*

Val: "I said to my son: 'I'm getting older too,' and he looked at me with total astonishment."

Monica: "They think of me as the one who looks after everybody else. I'm always ok. It would not occur to them to say - are you all right?"

Mary: "I said, do you realise that I have visited my mum every day for twenty-five years? And he said, isn't that lovely! Does he make an effort to see me? He phones once a week from the car and thinks he has done his duty."

Susie: "She likes to think we are all right."

It was not always clear in those interviews whether the problem of support going in mainly one direction was a structural one, with rigidly assigned role expectations between the generations, or whether it was problem of communication, in that mothers were often not clear enough in their communication of needing to be considered and cared for. Either way, there seemed to be a deep ambivalence about this in some of the mothers. They might wish for their child to consider their needs, but they also wish to hold on to their identity as mothers which they often define as being strong and being the *source* of support.

Sheila: *"I don't like to be seen as weak."*

As the short story "In the vulnerable group" suggests, being seen as vulnerable is by no means a desirable state. Accepting vulnerability, particularly a vulnerability that comes with growing old, is a very difficult and multi-dimensional process. It may well be easier to hold on to an image of everlasting strength, even if it is at times burdensome, as long as it allows one to avoid facing up to one's own vulnerability and the inevitable challenge of old age. For the adult child it is one thing to fight a strong parent, it is quite another to deal with having won. For generational succession to take place the old have to go, but this is a difficult victory for the young. The young man who realises he could now beat his father who he always viewed as a strong man, or the young woman who notices that her infuriatingly powerful mother has become frail, will on the whole experience this as a moment of shock rather than triumph. For the ageing mother it is one thing to wish for her child to be more mindful of her needs and more supportive, but it is quite another to realise that this involves having to accept care and possibly lose independence and a view of oneself as strong and competent. Both adult children and their parents may be engaged in a dance of denial that on some level suits them both, because dealing with the reality of the change is just too difficult.

There is no doubt that having grown-up children, and particularly having grandchildren, reminds us powerfully that we are now the older generation. For some mothers in my interviews this was brought home particularly poignantly by events that happened in parallel: the death of their own remaining parents or the onset of physical conditions for their partners or themselves that are associated with old age. Even for those mothers who still felt adventurous and physically fit, becoming older or being perceived as older was talked about directly or at times hinted at in the interviews.

> Helen: "*Looking after the grandchildren is fun, but I am so exhausted afterwards, it is frightening!*"

> Debbie: "*Health starts to become an issue, first with your parents, then perhaps with your partner, with yourself.*"

> Jacqueline: "*My mother told me there is no joy in getting old... I am fighting age, I don't want to be old, I keep working... of course you cannot turn the clock back.*"

> Sheila: "*The grandchildren are getting older, soon they will be doing their own thing. I am getting older, there is less I can do, there is less I do that is of interest to them.*"

Jan: *"We are getting older, I am aware our resources are getting more limited, the time we have got left, the energy. You become more aware of your own mortality and that of your partner... we get older in different ways, my husband is now watching elderly quiz shows!"*

As pointed out before, old age does not have positive connotations in Western culture. In a recent conversation on *Gransnet* a woman complained that she had been getting used to having a nap in the afternoon and sleeping in in the mornings during the pandemic and this had made her feel so old. This was followed by posts which bemoaned "feeling old", citing various other characteristics of that state including lack of energy, lack of curiosity, lack of focus, lack of sense of fun, not taking care of oneself, all of them, without exception, negative. One participant interestingly reframed sleeping-in and lack of structure and routine as making her feel "like a student", thus turning it into something positive, but only at the price of dropping the label "old". I was reminded of this recently: during the pandemic, prompted by the lack of opportunities to go to the hairdresser, I had finally done what I had thought about for a while. I had stopped dying my hair and allowed myself to go grey. One day I opened the door to the postman who had not seen me for a while and who told me cheerfully that, whilst he did not regard my grey hair as a problem, it definitely made me look older. What is interesting in this context is the implicit assumption in that comment that I would not want to look older and therefore hurry back to my previous younger looks. What does it mean to look old or "your age"? Why is it that to be told that one looks younger is still seen as a compliment? Why did his comment not only infuriate me but, if I am honest, also unsettle me for a little while?

Facing up to growing older involves a lot more than decisions as to whether to go grey or not. Several mothers in my interviews were actively thinking about the next stage of their life that may involve needing more support from their children or other people.

Moving house at this stage for example is often considered in the context of finding a place that will be convenient for growing old in. Some parents move towards their children, sometimes in some more or less unspoken understanding that they will be available to help their adult child with childcare now, but that some support may be available to the grandparents at some later stage in life if the need arises. Indeed this prospect raises difficult questions. With increasing life expectancy, there is a greater likelihood of the mother becoming more vulnerable in old age and her need for support growing accordingly. This would change the balance of need and support dramatically. Some generations ago there would have been a clear expectation that the younger generation would actively be involved in the care of the elderly. This expectation has changed a great deal, though again culturally different backgrounds lead to a range of different expectations. Taking care of the older generation seems to still form a strong expectation in families whose cultural expectation does not define "family" in the Western sense of the nuclear family. If this care cannot be provided, if for example not all generations live in the same country, then feelings of guilt are the norm.

> Nita: *"We go and visit my parents often, but I know I cannot be there for them the way I should as their daughter. My life is here, my children are here, but my parents are there and they are getting more and more frail. I just cannot see a solution."*

When asking mothers what their own expectations of being cared for by their adult children were, most of differentiated between providing personal care and giving support. Nearly all of them said they would not want their child to provide direct personal care, but hoped for other forms of support.

> Val: *"I didn't have my children so they would look after me in old age."*

Mary: *"I would want my children to care about me and not care for me."*

A formulation I often heard was not wanting to be a burden:

"I would not want to be a burden and spoil the relationship."

Often memories of having to provide care for elderly relatives or having witnessed this in the family influences this attitude. In general they agree that things have changed:

Sheila: *"When I was a child both of my grandmothers were cared for by aunts. I can't recall there being resentment about providing care either. Changing expectations are just a sign of the times."*

When it comes to being more specific about what kind of support they may want for themselves, visits are mentioned, maybe support in finding a good care home, help with paperwork or financial management:

Sharon: *"I hope they would support us with visits, with phone calls, come round with a cake and a bottle."*

Susie: *"I do not want personal care but I do want some attention."*

At times there is considerable anxiety shining through:

Monica: *"The idea of being looked after by them fills me with horror. I have always been independent, always been a bit of a control freak."*

There is also tongue-in-cheek advice:

"Hope for support but make plans!"

In general it proved difficult to draw out mothers to engage in this part of the interviews. This was not something they wanted to think about and sometimes there was nearly a block to imagining oneself in that situation. Old age and mortality were now on the map, but few of them wanted to think too much about it. Not Yet!

For all of my interviewees the phase of old age when one might not be able to look after oneself was still in the future, thought about, but not experienced yet. The closest they came to what it may actually be like to be in that state came from observations of their own parents: they talked of observing their parents' pride, their at times desperate attempts to hold on to some independence, their rage at feeling patronised by their however well-meaning children. My interviewees observed, empathised, became exasperated, felt guilty and conflicted about being dragged into a position where they "had to be the adult", sometimes directly having to make decisions, for example about a parent's move to a care home. There was no doubt that all of them who were in this position were acutely aware of the fact that it might be them next, with a parent's death often removing the last protective layer between themselves in the middle generation to becoming part of the old generation. They knew!

Old age is sometimes described as a succession of stages, "young" old age, "middle" old age and "old" old age. Throughout these stages old age brings with it many challenges, many of them physical, but also cognitive, emotional and social. Stiff joints, dodgy short-term memory, changing energy levels are just part of the story. Old age also means that we may lose friends and partners, that we may be treated with disrespect or just sheer disinterest and may be made to feel increasingly irrelevant. It is characterised by many losses and can for some of us feel very lonely. Yet it also gives us perspective, space, a sense of priorities and an ability to be mindful of the time-limitedness of everything. For women who have had children and whose children have grown up this time-limitedness is very much part of their experience:

where did those years go? Now that they have the time and space to focus back on themselves they find themselves to have changed and to be growing old. The stepping back that their children demand is paralleled by a stepping back from their own youth and finding a different way of being themselves: to be approaching old age and not to be afraid of it.

What to do and who to be

- Try to be honest with yourself about the reality of growing older. This is one of the crucial factors that accompanies the growing up of our children. The loss that you may be feeling is intrinsically linked with the change you know you are yourself undergoing. Try not to avoid this however hard it may feel.

- Growing older is not always easy but it is up to you how you approach this. The more you can find a creative and positive attitude to the change in yourself, the more you are likely to be creative and positive about the inevitable changes in your relationship with your child.

- Do not feel afraid: old age is not for the fainthearted, but neither does it need to be the grim, feeble spectre that we are sold. Define it yourself! That does not mean pretending not to be old. We cannot defy age, but we can defy the stereotypes that come with it. "Gay" used to be a term of abuse and was then appropriated by the gay community as a term of pride. How about recapturing the term "old" for ourselves? Could we learn to be "proud to be old"?

Summary and conclusions

I have been delaying writing this chapter. It is never the easiest part of a book to gather the different strands and pull out the core points made.

However I do not think my reluctance to approach it is entirely due to this. The conversations I have had with my interviewees, the literature that I have read have been accompanied by events in my own life that are relevant to the subject matter this book deals with.

There has been a pandemic. Like everybody else I was physically cut off for a long time from many people that mattered to me. Friends, family, patients I could only see online, reduced to endless Zoom calls interrupted by dodgy internet connections. Many of them live in different countries and the interruption of physical contact continues while I am writing this. My mother died during this time in a care home in Germany and I had not been able to visit her for several months leading up to her death. I only managed to attend her small, socially distanced and masked funeral. I could not go to a memorial event for my half-brother in the USA later that year. Just before the first lockdown my son split up from his longstanding partner who I loved dearly. I worked hard on keeping in touch with my granddaughter who turned two during the first lockdown and who, on our first real meeting in an outdoor space midway between her home and ours, was clearly anxious about not touching us. She had understood something about the danger we might pose to each other. My second granddaughter was born during the second lockdown, or was it the third lockdown? Or the fourth? I am not sure how we all would have coped without support bubbles being officially allowed by that stage.

Why is this relevant?

Firstly, it highlighted the importance of these connections and how they shape and maintain who I am. The effort we all made to keep linked up with each other, the sharp and acute need to "stay in touch" that I heard my patients talk about and that I experienced myself confirmed what I was writing about; namely that we are indeed creatures who exist in social systems that feed us, that can nourish us and help us to be who we are and want to be, but at the same time can hurt us and disturb us. It also confirmed that these systems overlap and we turn to friends sometimes, to partners sometimes, to family sometimes and make ourselves available to them in that same changing and shifting way. We are who we are because of what we are part of.

Our families are clearly a crucial part of this. They are a place where intimacy, regression and very complex emotions reign to an extent that is rarely present in adult friendships, however deep. They are also laden with history and they follow us throughout our life, even if intensity and frequency of contact may change a lot over time. We are somebody's child and our relationship with our parents will have a powerful impact on the person we are and the kind of relationships we form and can tolerate in later contexts.

We may also become somebody's parent and that will change things for the rest of our lives. When I found out I was pregnant with my first child one of the first thoughts that went through my mind was that from now on it could never again be just about me. That was over. And from then on being a mother never stops: once a mother, always a mother, indeed! But, and here comes the big but: being a mother changes constantly and writing this book has made me more aware of the nature and magnitude of this change than I had been before.

I have now read a lot about family relationships, about ageing, about being female in a society in which being a woman and also old invites disturbing and difficult attitudes. I have interviewed women about their experience of being a mother while growing older and negotiating the relationship with adult children. I have experienced some of it myself. What are my conclusions?

1. The first point I have been trying to make is this: becoming a mother changes our identity and our relationships in a most profound way. Whatever follows, however our relationship with our children develops, even if we lose a child or there is an estrangement between them and us, we never cease to be mothers. Being a mother redraws our internal map of the world and who we are in it. Whether we love our children or not, whether we are "good" or "bad" mothers, whether we maintain our relationships with them into their adult lives or not, whether we regard these relationships as satisfactory or not, whatever the nature of our attachment to them and theirs is to us, once we have become mothers this change of the internal map is not reversible.

2. The second point is that the nature of our involvement with our children is one that is constantly changing. The years of active mothering during our children's early childhood demand different ways of engaging than do the years of their adolescence, the young adult having flown the nest will pose different challenges from the one who settles back at home. Whether our child is single or with a partner, whether they are financially independent, whether they become parents themselves, whether they run their lives competently or not, all these factors will influence what is demanded of us as mothers or indeed what we may demand of ourselves. The rules of engagement are in constant flux.

3. The third point is that change leads to transitions and transitions are hard work. They point backwards and nearly always involve loss and having to let go of something. They also point forwards and demand that we adapt to a new situation and engage with it in a productive way. Becoming a mother is a powerful challenge and years of early mothering are characterised by the pressure and pleasure of being at the centre of a small child's world, crucial to their evolving physical and emotional survival. The task of creating a relationship in which successful and secure attachment can be formed is at the core of this. Everything else develops from this base, and yet the emphasis shifts increasingly towards facilitating the child's independence away from mother. Where mothers were once core *participants* in their children's lives, they now, with their child's growing independence, have to gradually get used to becoming *observers* of their child's lives. They have to move from the centre to the margins. This will involve losses and it will not always be emotionally easy to cope with this shift and the accompanying feelings that may include exclusion, jealousy, rejection and grief about feeling the loss of importance and usefulness. It may also be liberating and a relief and allow mothers to define what they want the next chapter of their lives to look like.

4. My fourth point is that at the core of being a mother of an adult child there is the ongoing negotiation of closeness and distance between mothers and children. Intimacy and close attachment should form the base from which separation and independence develop, which in turn allow for a new way of adult relating. This negotiation is constantly going on, with flashpoints around young adults leaving home, bringing new partners back into the family and becoming parents themselves, all of which

ask for major adjustments of the relationship between mother and adult child. In the experience of mothers what is most visible is the fact that they see their child in charge of this process. The adult child calls the shots as far as these negotiations are concerned and mothers see themselves as responding to their child's agenda.

5. The fifth point is that the changing identity as a mother, as mapped on the developmental stages of her child moving into adulthood, is accompanied by the mother's attitude towards her own past and future life. She may enjoy the chance to reengage with her pre-mother self on the one hand and on the other hand she has to deal with the reality of moving through middle age into old age. Whatever the quality of her relationship with her child and however satisfactorily those negotiations mentioned above are developing, she has at the same time to find a way of dealing with her own ageing and her own mortality. This becomes evident around the arrival of grandchildren, around the death of her own parents and finally in her own attitude to becoming older and in the physical, social and emotional challenges that this brings. This has a profound impact on how she will engage with her child's adult life.

6. How mothers find their way through this maze is dependent on many factors. Societal and cultural factors shape our expectations. Economic and educational factors will influence what our options are. Societies that place greater emphasis on the extended multigenerational family allow older mothers a greater role and often a higher status. Western emphasis on the core nuclear two generation family allocates mothers a more distanced place from their adult children and consequently demands a greater degree of stepping

back and becoming an observer. Cultural stereotypes will leave their imprint on our expectations of how we should behave and how we will be perceived as mothers-in-law and grandmothers, whether we ever consciously think about that or not. Societal attitudes to ageing and to older women may make this journey complicated well beyond the set-up of our individual families. We may not be consciously aware of these stereotypes, but they will be reflected in our anxieties and expectations which in turn will influence how we allow ourselves to behave.

7. As a psychotherapist I am also aware of the power of individual *internal* factors, such as transgenerational patterns of behaving and feeling in any particular family. Each mother will have her own demons, but also her own coping mechanisms that will influence how she can make her way through this maze. She will have her very own personal blueprint of how to be a participant or observer and how she feels about it. This blueprint will have formed in her own early life and will influence how she deals with this family transition. Often these factors are at play outside of our awareness, but they can lead to repetitive patterns in families.

8. For years the struggle will be to establish an adult relationship with our grown-up children in which a greater degree of mutuality is established. Just as the move from participant to observer is one that will change and shift constantly, so is the move from always "being mother" to one where both parties can relate to each other as people in a mutual and reciprocal way. It demands constant adjustment and was rarely described by any mother as a fixed state, some finding it forever elusive. Ultimately, with advancing years mothers also have to accept that their relationship with their adult

child will need to include a certain reversal of roles. The adult child will "become mother". This means dealing with one's own increasing vulnerability and coping with one's children's response to this.

9. There are things we can do to help ourselves in order to make these transitions easier or harder. As so often in the context of family relationships, and in mothering in particular, our worst obstacles are associated with perfectionism and shame. Perfectionism can set impossibly high standards that are bound to make us feel we fail. Shame as a result of that sense of failing can make us hide our feelings and present a different picture to the outside world, thereby increasing the sense of isolation. To interrupt this cycle the first step is to acknowledge how fiendishly difficult these transitions are. To understand that grief and conflict are a normal part of what we are experiencing is the second one. A third step is to embrace the notion of "good enough" mothering that allows for difficulties, conflict, and getting it wrong to be an inevitable part of the job description. A fourth step is to embrace our non-mother identity and refocus energy and emotional investment, so that we are not tied into a relationship with our children where they have to be everything for us.

The word journey tends to be rather overused, but I cannot find a better one: motherhood is indeed a journey, across some wondrous and at times thorny terrain. I watched my daughter pack her overnight bag for the hospital prior to the birth of her first child, getting ready for the ride, and I felt an awe that I felt over and over again when I listened to my interviewees. What a ride! Hold on tight, I wanted to say to my daughter, this is going to be the trip of a lifetime! Welcome!

Acknowledgements

I would like to thank all women whose stories led to this book, especially my interviewees who were very generous in sharing their memories, thoughts and feelings.

There also have been many women in my life, family, friends and patients who over the years have taught me a lot. Being a mother is an experience that should not be undertaken on our own and other women and their take on it has been invaluable. Thank you for doing this with me and feeling it with me and thinking about it with me without flinching. This book would never have existed without you. Thank you to all those of you who have been reading drafts, for offering comments, but most of all for engaging together with me in the subject matter and encouraging me in the belief that I may have something to say on it. Thank you, Christine Bornhak, Chris Bunday, Ceri Dunn, Gillian Isaacs Russell, Elizabeth Marks, Mechthild Rueller, Ulla Schwetlick, Moira Stevenson, Patrick Stevenson, Fiona Thompson and Carol Topolski.

In particular I would like to mention Wendy Gracias with whom I have lived motherhood from the beginnings and who has been a wonderful friend and thought provoking writing companion. How many times can you talk with somebody about the same thing and something else becomes visible and clearer? Here is to many more walks by the sea!

Thank you also to my writing buddy Jeanne Moulton, for detailed comments and encouragements, and to my sister Regina who proved that she is indeed the one with the talent for languages by reading the whole manuscript in her fourth language with the help of a dictionary. And then appropriately corrected my English!

Thank you also to my sister-in-law Jill Brook for spotting that tiny detail. You know the one I mean.

Thank you to Alice Solomons and Lisa Findley at Free Association Books, for encouragement, cooperative editing and of course for taking me on for a second time.

Thank you to Anna, Chris and Sam for their patience and encouragement. May I ask for one more thing: could you keep your amusement at my advice sections within limits?

And thank you in particular to John, who not only went tirelessly through edit after edit, but more importantly has now for several decades lived the book with me. Let's do the next chapters together, in and out of comfort zones!

Annette Byford has worked as a psychologist and psychotherapist in private practice for the last 25 years and as a lecturer and supervisor in various settings (university, NHS, and the voluntary sector). She is a chartered counselling psychologist and a senior practitioner on the Register of Psychologists specialising in Psychotherapy.